YORK NOTES

Macbeth

William Shakespeare

Note by Alasdair D.F. Macrae

Longman   York Press

Exterior picture of the Globe Theatre reproduced by permission of the
Raymond Mander and Joe Mitchenson Theatre Collection
Reconstruction of the Globe Theatre interior reprinted from Hodges:
The Globe Restored (1968) by permission of Oxford University Press

Alasdair D. F. Macrae is hereby identified as author of this work in accordance
with Section 77 of the Copyright, Designs and Patents Act 1988

YORK PRESS
322 Old Brompton Road, London SW5 9JH

PEARSON EDUCATION LIMITED
Edinburgh Gate, Harlow,
Essex CM20 2JE, United Kingdom
Associated companies, branches and representatives throughout the world

First published 2001

ISBN 0-582-42473-9

Designed by Vicki Pacey
Phototypeset by Gem Graphics, Trenance, Mawgan Porth, Cornwall
Colour reproduction and film output by Spectrum Colour
Produced by Addison Wesley Longman China Limited, Hong Kong

CONTENTS

PART ONE

INTRODUCTION

HOW TO STUDY A PLAY

Studying on your own requires self-discipline and a carefully thought-out work plan in order to be effective.

- Drama is a special kind of writing (the technical term is '**genre**') because it needs a performance in the theatre to arrive at a full interpretation of its meaning. Try to imagine that you are a member of the audience when reading the play. Think about how it could be presented on the stage, not just about the words on the page.

- Drama is often about conflict of some sort (which may be below the surface). Identify the conflicts in the play and you will be close to identifying the large ideas or themes which bind all the parts together.

- Make careful notes on themes, character, plot and any subplots of the play.

- Why do you like or dislike the characters in the play? How do your feelings towards them develop and change?

- Playwrights find non-realistic ways of allowing an audience to see into the minds and motives of their characters, for example **soliloquy**, aside or music. Consider how such dramatic devices are used in the play.

- Think of the playwright writing the play. Why were these particular arrangements of events, characters and speeches chosen?

- Cite exact sources for all quotations, whether from the text itself or from critical commentaries. Wherever possible find your own examples from the play to back up your own opinions.

- Always express your ideas in your own words.

This York Note offers an introduction to *Macbeth* and cannot substitute for close reading of the text and the study of secondary sources.

Macbeth is probably the most widely read and seen of William Shakespeare's plays. One of his shortest, it has a focus and succinctness which fit an uncluttered plot and highlight what seem to be straightforward moral dilemmas. Although the story is set in a specific historical period and place, the themes are of universal interest and relevance, themes such as ambition, loyalty, treachery, conscience, delusion, social and psychological order, the struggle of good and evil, and what is ultimately valuable in human life. The story itself, with one exceptional deviation, has a clear shape with distinct stages and a firm ending; there are fights, murders, witches, ghosts and nightmares among its sensational ingredients. With very few main characters and no sub-plot, it is easily held in the mind of the reader.

The play's memorability and adaptability have resulted in it being produced in innumerable versions across the world. Apart from the more obvious stage and film productions, there have been numerous adaptations. Verdi's opera *Macbeth* is a favourite in the opera repertoire; and some of the more famous films based on the play include the Hollywood gangster movie *Joe Macbeth* (1955) set in Chicago with a gangland climax and *Throne of Blood* (1957) by the Japanese director Akira Kurosawa set in a medieval Japan of warlords engaged in a struggle for domination. In British theatres, *Macbeth* has, for all its popularity, come to be associated with a superstition of bad luck, and actors and stage workers avoid referring to the play by its name when it is in production.

PART TWO

Summaries

Macbeth was first published in 1623 in what is known as the First Folio, a collection of all but one (*Pericles*) of Shakespeare's plays made by John Heminges and Henry Condell, who had known and acted with Shakespeare for twenty years. The text of *Macbeth* in the First Folio is very close to what we read in a modern edition of the play. However, the text of a Shakespeare play as we read it now is the result of careful work by many editors in the intervening years. Even in the case of *Macbeth*, not a difficult play editorially compared with some, editors have to make choices. For example, in the Folio, Act I Scene 7, Macbeth says to Lady Macbeth

> I dare do all that may become a man;
> Who dares no more, is none (lines 46–7)

An editor over 250 years ago suggested that 'do' makes easier sense than 'no' in line 47 and his suggestion has been accepted generally ever since. Some editors have doubted the genuineness of certain scenes, in particular the Porter scene in Act II Scene 3 and some of the Witches' appearances. The spelling, stage directions and line and even scene divisions are not always the same from one edition to another.

We know for certain that *Macbeth* was performed in 1611 because a very full eye-witness account survives. All the evidence available to us suggests that *Macbeth* was first performed in 1606, possibly in front of King James himself. The play was seriously altered in 1663 to bring it more into line with the taste of the period and this rather operatic version with songs and dances survived into the nineteenth century.

The edition used in this Note is the New Penguin Shakespeare edition of *Macbeth*, edited by G.K. Hunter. In the revised edition (1995), Hunter offers a substantial account of the text.

The authority of Duncan, King of Scotland, is under threat from rebellions by some of his nobles and attacks by invading Vikings. Macbeth, Thane of Glamis, emerges as the fiercest warrior in support of his king and is rewarded with the added title of Thane of Cawdor. The Witches appear to be able to anticipate events before they actually happen, and they lead Macbeth and Banquo to believe that greater honours lie ahead for them, in Macbeth's case the crown of Scotland. Macbeth takes their predictions very seriously and, when Duncan comes to spend the night with him in his castle, his wife, who has been informed of the predictions, urges Macbeth to seize the opportunity to eliminate the king. This is done by a very nervous Macbeth but Lady Macbeth has to complete the job by placing the blood-covered daggers beside Duncan's servants and smearing them with the blood. When the king's murdered body is discovered in the early morning, Macbeth kills the servants in an apparent fit of righteous outrage, Duncan's sons, Malcolm and Donalbain, fearing for their lives, flee and Macbeth is crowned as the new king. Because the Witches have predicted that Banquo's offspring will become kings, Macbeth decides to have Banquo and his only son, Fleance, murdered. Banquo is killed but Fleance escapes. At a banquet, hosted by the new king and queen, Macbeth receives news of Banquo's death and Fleance's escape; immediately the ghost of Banquo appears to Macbeth, terrifying him and disrupting the banquet. In Scotland rumours of plots and conspiracies abound and there is a general sense of corruption and fear. Macbeth seeks out the Witches but receives very ambiguous messages from them, which only encourage his suspicious nature. When word comes that Macduff, Thane of Fife, has left Scotland either in flight or to seek help against Macbeth from the English king, Macbeth orders Macduff's family to be murdered. Macduff receives news of their death while he is in discussion at the English court with Malcolm, Duncan's exiled son. They agree to lead an army against Macbeth. Back in Scotland, Lady Macbeth's mental stability has collapsed in guilt and Macbeth is deserted by many of his previous supporters. As his castle at Dunsinane comes under increased attack, he is told of his wife's suicide and now, virtually alone, he stands against his attackers. Macduff finally manages to kill him and, in front of Macbeth's severed head, Malcolm is declared King of Scotland.

ACT I

Three Witches are gathered in an open place in a thunder storm. They agree to re-assemble on the moorland before sunset to meet Macbeth.

The opening scene of a play is particularly important in establishing a mood or atmosphere in which the main action of the play will be seen by the audience. The scene is set in 'an open place', a place removed from the ordinary business of men and the usual social rules. The weather is extravagant and hostile to men, the 'fog and filthy air' suggesting unusual darkness and unhealthiness. The conversation of the Witches is again removed from the interchange of ordinary men; the use of rhyme is a feature of the Witches' speech and throughout the play it intensifies a sense of incantation, of magical charms. In line 4, 'When the battle's lost and won' and line 9, 'Fair is foul, and foul is fair' a curious paradox is offered. How can a battle be lost *and* won? How can fair be foul? What are opposites for us seem to be interchangeable for the Witches. And there is the appearance of the Witches themselves, traditionally ugly, barely human, often taking the shape of animals like cats and toads. Every detail of the short opening scene urges our imagination to sense a confusion of the usual human order, a reverse of human values, a world of darkness and foulness, a sinister challenge to ordinary goodness. And in the middle of the scene comes the startling line 'There to meet with Macbeth.' What can Macbeth, whose name gives the play its title, have to do with these abnormal, distasteful creatures? How does he fit in to their plans? They seem to know of the outcome of the battle before the battle is over.

3 **hurly-burly** turmoil, confusion
8 **Grey-Malkin** grey cat
Padock toad (Cats and toads were the animals most commonly associated with witches and it was thought that witches could adopt the shapes or voices of these animals)
Anon at once

SCENE 2

Duncan and others are in an army camp receiving reports of the battles fought against him by an alliance of Sweno, King of Norway, Macdonwald, Lord of the Western Isles of Scotland, and the Thane of Cawdor who has proved disloyal to King Duncan. The reports, direct from the fields of battle, all stress the heroism of Macbeth, one of Duncan's generals, in ensuring the victory of the king's cause. Duncan, in gratitude for the victory, announces that Macbeth is to be given the title of Thane of Cawdor and the treacherous Cawdor is to be executed immediately.

The military alarum (sound of trumpets) is in contrast to the thunder and lightning of the first scene and the play shifts from the wild world of the Witches to the place where the royal authority is demonstrated. The focus of our attention in this scene is on Macbeth and on his virtues as a loyal soldier to King Duncan. The battle is given a size and an importance which magnify the qualities of Macbeth. Duncan has nothing but praise for the heroic deeds of Macbeth. Our curiosity and anticipation are aroused to meet this mighty champion so praised by all who have seen him. But our memories still hold the mention of his name by the Witches and the final line of the scene reminds us of line 4 in Scene 1 and this connection is consolidated in Scene 3.

3 **newest state** latest news

7 **broil** struggle

9 **choke their art** make it impossible for either to swim

10–12 **for to ... upon him** because, for that purpose, the innumerable nasty qualities (or people) crowd and grow on him like vermin

13 **kerns and galloglasses** lightly armed soldiers and heavily armed soldiers

15 **Showed ... whore** appeared to favour Macdonwald but, like a prostitute, proved unreliable

all's too weak all his efforts were inadequate

19 **valour's minion** the favourite of bravery (that is, Macbeth)

21 **Which** who

22 **unseamed ... chops** split Macdonwald from his navel to his jaws

24 **cousin** a common term of endearment in Elizabethan English but Macbeth was Duncan's cousin in the modern sense

25 **As ... reflection** just as when the sun is bright too early (and the subsequent day is stormy and disappointing)

27 **spring** source, early situation

30 **skipping** light-footed

trust their heels rely on flight

31 **surveying vantage** sensing an opportunity

32 **furbished** polished or provided

36 **say sooth** speak truthfully

37 **overcharged ... cracks** loaded with double charges of explosive

39 **Except** unless

40 **reeking** smoking, steaming (compare line 18)

41 **memorize another Golgotha** making the place as famous for slaughter as Golgotha (Hebrew word meaning place of the skulls), the site of Calvary where Christ was crucified

46 **smack of** indicate

47 **Thane** title of nobility in Scotland

51 **Norweyan** Norwegian, Viking

flout wave in defiance

52 **fan ... cold** make the people cold with fear

53 **Norway** the King of Norway

56 **Bellona** Roman goddess of war

lapped in proof dressed in tested armour

57 **confronted ... self-comparisons** faced him as an equal

58 **Point** sword

59 **lavish** insolent

62 **composition** terms of peace

64 **disbursèd** paid

Saint Colm's Inch Island of Inchcolm near Edinburgh

65 **dollars** coins (not actually in existence at the time of Macbeth)

67 **bosom** closest, dearest

present immediate

SCENE 3

The Witches recount the dreadful things they can do to men. As Macbeth and Banquo enter on their way home from their victory, the Witches prepare themselves with a charm. When challenged by the

generals, the Witches greet Macbeth as Thane of Glamis, Thane of
Cawdor and king to be, and Banquo is told that he will produce heirs
who will become kings. The Witches disappear just before Ross and
Angus arrive to announce that the king has conferred on Macbeth the
title of Thane of Cawdor. Macbeth speculates to himself on what the
future may hold for him and proposes to Banquo that they find time later
to discuss the strange happening.

In the first two scenes of the play, the world of the Witches has
been separated from the world of men. Now these two worlds are
brought together. The Witches' conversation emphasises that their
evil and vindictive will cannot be thwarted by men. Their curse on
the sea-captain can be read as a prediction of Macbeth's career. The
rhymed incantation of the Witches' speech is again obvious.
Macbeth's first line in the play arrests us because it is so close to
the manner of the Witches and we remember, consciously or not,
the end of Scene 1. The Witches answer Macbeth rather than
Banquo and his reaction to the greeting of the Witches is quite
different from that of Banquo; Macbeth is perturbed and
frightened: Banquo is calm and sceptical. The confirmation of
Macbeth as Thane of Cawdor adds to the puzzlement of Macbeth
and Banquo, who is concerned that men are easily tempted into sin
by the 'instruments of darkness'. In his **asides**, Macbeth reveals a
deeply disturbed mind; something in himself seems to have been
echoed in the Witches' words and it is this exposure of his inner
mind that gives him most concern. Furthermore, if the Witches
have been proved right about the Thane of Cawdor, then the next
stage may be inevitable. Or, does he have to act? In the first scene
in which he appears, Macbeth reveals a strong power of
imagination and even at this early stage he tries to deceive people
(see lines 149–50).

6 **Aroint thee** get off!
  rump-fed ronyon fat-bottomed slut
7 *Tiger* there was an actual ship of this name which returned in 1606 after a
  bad voyage
8 **sieve** witches defied the laws of nature
9 **rat ... tail** witches took the shape of animals but not the tail

10 **I'll do** I'll deal with him

15–17 **ports ... card** she controls all the winds and can cause them to blow from whichever unfavourable direction of the compass she chooses

20 **penthouse lid** eyelid (like a sloping roof)

21 **forbid** accursed

24 **peak** grow thinner

 pine waste away

25 **bark** ship

31 **Weird** the old English word for destiny

32 **Posters** fast travellers

36 **wound up** prepared, complete

38 **is't called** is it said to be

43 **choppy** rough and cut

52 **fantastical** imaginary

54 **present grace** Thane of Glamis

54–5 **prediction ... having** Thane of Cawdor

55 **royal hope** the throne of Scotland

56 **rapt** entranced, spellbound

70 **Sinell** Macbeth's father

80 **corporal** bodily, material

83 **insane root** some narcotic plant

97 **post** messenger

103 **earnest** pledge

105 **addition** title

108 **borrowed robes** the garments (and qualities) of another person

111 **line** support

112 **vantage** opportunity

113 **wrack** destruction

114 **capital** most serious

116 **behind** still to come

119 **home** completely

120 **enkindle** encourage you to hope

125 **consequence** seriousness

127 **swelling** magnificent (the image is from the theatre)

129 **soliciting** offer, invitation

135 **seated** fixed

139 **single state** whole being

140 **function** the ability to act

   surmise speculation

141 **nothing ... not** the future, the imagined has cancelled out the present, the
   actual

143 **will have me** intends me to be

144 **my stir** me doing anything

145 **strange** new

   cleave ... mould fit the wearer

146–7 **Come ... day** whatever is going to happen will happen whatever the day
   looks like

148 **stay ... leisure** await your convenience

149 **favour** pardon

   wrought troubled

150–2 **your pains ... read them** in his memory

153 **at more ... it** later, when we have had time to consider the matter

155 **free hearts** honest feelings

SCENE 4

In the palace at Forres, Duncan hears his son, Malcolm, relate how the
treacherous Cawdor has been executed. Macbeth enters and is warmly
welcomed by the king. Banquo is also commended. Duncan announces
that Malcolm is to be the heir to the throne and confers on him the title
of Prince of Cumberland. When Duncan voices his intention to travel to
Inverness (Macbeth's castle), Macbeth sets out to take the news to his
wife and prepare a welcome for his king. Macbeth realises that the new
Prince of Cumberland is an obstacle to his ambition and proposes to act
quickly.

We are presented with a picture of royal order and justice. The
portrait of the dying Cawdor as penitent and dignified is placed
against the arrival of Macbeth. Duncan shows himself to be an
innocent and trusting person and addresses Macbeth as 'worthiest
cousin'. Macbeth answers Duncan's thanks and praise in an
obedient but ornate manner. Notice the emphasis on 'service',
'loyalty', 'owe', 'your highness', 'duties', 'state', 'safe', 'love', 'honour'
– all in half a dozen lines. Macbeth's words suggest a model of the
loyal subject but already we know something of another side to

Macbeth. Banquo thanks the king by merely completing the **metaphor** (of growing) used by Duncan. Shakespeare's choice of this moment for Duncan to name his successor is very shrewd dramatically. Duncan's announcement forces Macbeth's mind further into his thoughts of the previous scene and when Duncan indicates that he will spend the night in Macbeth's castle we suspect hollowness and untrustworthiness in Macbeth's saying:

I'll be myself the harbinger, and make joyful
The hearing of my wife with your approach (lines 46–7)

In his **aside** Macbeth invokes darkness to hide his intentions and we think back to the 'instruments of darkness' of the previous scene. The stars which are likened by Duncan to 'signs of nobleness' (line 42), are extinguished at Macbeth's command (line 51).

s.d. **Flourish** fanfare (of trumpets)
2 **in commission** authorised to conduct the execution
3 **liege** lord
9 **Became him** suited him, did him honour
10 **that ... studied** who had learned a part (like an actor)
11 **owed** owned
   careless worthless
11–12 **There's no art ... face** there is no certain way of knowing a man's character from his face
20 **proportion** balance (as of money in a bank)
27 **Which do** the duties do
28 **Safe** entirely
32 **enfold** embrace
35 **Wanton** unrestrained
36 **drops of sorrow** tears of joy
38 **establish our estate** settle the succession (to the throne of Scotland)
41 **unaccompanied invest** exclusively apply to
44 **bind ... you** put us deeper in your debt
45 **The rest ... you** leisure is a burden if it is not employed to prepare for you
46 **harbinger** messenger (originally an official sent ahead to arrange accommodation for the king)
53 **wink at** be blind to

> **let that be** let that action be done
> 56 **in ... am fed** I am filled by praising him
> 59 **kinsman** Macbeth is Duncan's first cousin

SCENE 5

In Inverness Castle Lady Macbeth is reading a letter sent to her by Macbeth after he had met the Witches but before he met Duncan. Lady Macbeth's mind immediately looks forward to the fulfilment of the Witches' prophecy but she feels that Macbeth is too mild to seize the throne. A messenger arrives with the news that Duncan plans to spend the night in the Castle and, by the time her husband enters, Lady Macbeth has already prepared her mind for the murder of Duncan. Macbeth wavers but Lady Macbeth's resolution is absolute.

> There is no preparation of the audience for the character of Macbeth's wife. She appears in this scene as a ruthless, totally committed woman whose every effort is to strive for the greater glory of her husband. Macbeth's tendency to speculate and think round problems, a quality we noted in Scene 3, is seen by his wife as a crucial weakness. He does not lack ambition but he is squeamish about the methods to be used to achieve this ambition. The hardness necessary for an assassination must come from her. There is an element in Lady Macbeth's attitude strongly reminiscent of the Witches; she talks of pouring her spirits in Macbeth's ear like some potion to alter his character and she invokes the spirits of evil to defeminise her, to dehumanise her, and like Macbeth in the previous scene, she prays for darkness to hide her planned action. The chain of imperatives ('come', 'fill', etc.) gives her speech a special urgency and determination. When Macbeth appears there is little trace of endearment from his wife. She sees him and forces him to see himself in terms of her plan for power. She addresses him as he had been addressed by the Witches in Scene 3 and there is a drastic brevity in her language: 'He that's coming must be provided for'. The arrival of the Messenger announcing Duncan's visit is a brilliant dramatic stroke. We know that Duncan is coming but what is so startling is the Messenger's arrival immediately after Lady Macbeth has voiced her plans. 'The

King comes here tonight' is the anticipation of her dearest wish. Even Lady Macbeth falters – for a moment.

2 **perfectest report** the best knowledge (either he has made enquiries about the Witches or his own experience has proved them right)

5 **missives** messengers

9 **deliver thee** report to you

10 **dues of rejoicing** appropriate joy

15 **milk of human-kindness** gentleness of decent humanity

18 **illness should attend it** necessary wickedness

18–19 **What thou ... holily** what you would like passionately to have, you would like to obtain by fair means

20–3 **Thou'dst have ... undone** you would like to have something (the crown) but it demands, 'You must do this' if you wish it, and you are more afraid to do this necessary job than eager to reverse it if it were actually done

24 **Hie** hasten

26 **chastise ... tongue** correct or strengthen with my strong words

27 **golden round** crown

28 **metaphysical** supernatural

31 **informed** sent word ahead

33 **had the speed of him** came faster than he did

36 **raven** bird announcing death

39 **mortal** deadly

40 **crown** top of her head

41 **thick** so that pity cannot pass to her heart

42 **remorse** compassion

43 **compunctions ... nature** natural feelings of pity

44 **fell** dreadful

44–5 **nor keep ... it** nor intervene between my intention and its fulfilment

46 **for gall** in exchange for sour vinegar
ministers evil spirits

47 **sightless** invisible

48 **wait on nature's mischief** attend on the disasters and evil possible in the world

49 **pall** wrap, hide as in a coffin cloth
dunnest darkest

53 **hereafter** of the future (the third prophecy)

55 **ignorant** unknowing

56 **instant** present

61 **to beguile ... time** to deceive people not to appear as they expect to see you

65 **provided for** dealt with (ironic way of saying killed)

66 **dispatch** care

69 **look up clear** appear cheerful

70 **To alter ... fear** to show a disturbed face is a betrayal of troubled thoughts

SCENE 6

Duncan and his attendant lords arrive at Macbeth's castle. While they are admiring the peaceful location of the castle they are welcomed by Lady Macbeth and she and Duncan exchange greetings and compliments.

The emphasis of this scene, as in Scene 4, is on peace, trust and courtesy. After the passion and vicious emotions of Scene 5 we are presented with images of tranquillity and the words 'guest' and 'host' are repeated. Lady Macbeth appears as the perfect, sophisticated hostess but we remember her advice to her husband:

look like the innocent flower,
But be the serpent under't (I.5.63–4)

The calm light of evening comes before the darkness of the following scenes.

s.d. **Hautboys** oboes

torches torchbearers

1 **seat** position

2 **Nimbly** freshly

3 **gentle** calm

4 **temple-haunting martlet** the house martin likes to nest in the eaves of tall buildings such as churches

approve prove

5 **By his loved mansionry** by building his nest here

6–7 **jutty, frieze, Buttress** architectural features that stick out from the walls

7 **coign of vantage** suitable corner

8 **pendent ... cradle** hanging nest for breeding in

9 **haunt** frequent

11 **The love ... trouble** he means that love can be burdensome in that it puts one in debt to the giver but it is, nonetheless, a great blessing

16 **single** feeble

business service, effort

19 **We rest your hermits** we still pray for you

21 **coursed** chased

22 **purveyor** the official who went ahead of the king to arrange his food

23 **holp** helped

25–8 **Your servants ... your own** she means that all that belongs to Macbeth really belongs to the king and he can claim any of it at any time

31 **By your leave** with your permission (he would kiss Lady Macbeth on the cheek)

SCENE 7

Macbeth has slipped out of the supper room and is having second thoughts on the plan to murder Duncan. He is aware of the seriousness of his proposed crime as an act of treachery against an innocent guest. When Lady Macbeth finds him, Macbeth has decided to cancel the plan but his wife persuades him to change his mind. She outlines her tactics and Macbeth cannot but admire her resolution. He steels himself for the murder.

Macbeth's final words in Scene 5 were, 'We will speak further'. His wavering then is continued in the present scene but when Lady Macbeth joins him they do not conduct a real discussion: she tells him what is to be done. Macbeth allows himself to imagine the future beyond the murder in a way which Lady Macbeth forbids herself. His will is weakened by speculation; her will is strengthened by a concentration on the act of killing Duncan. It is the difference between 'Why?' and 'How?'. Lady Macbeth's main argument is that her husband has to prove his manhood by acting decisively. Macbeth knows that there is another concept of man (lines 46–7) but he is dominated by a woman prepared to renounce the essence of her femininity until his argument is reduced to the cowardly line, 'If we should fail?'. Failure is not something that Lady Macbeth bothers to contemplate. In his final two speeches in the scene Macbeth adopts the manner of speaking of his wife and the echo of

Lady Macbeth's earlier sentiments (see Scene 5, lines 61–4) in his last couplet is not accidental. We remember also the significant line of the Witches in Scene 1 'Fair is foul, and foul is fair' and Macbeth's own 'So foul and fair a day I have not seen' (Scene 3, line 37) and we realise that the preparations are complete. We await the action.

s.d. **Sewer** the equivalent of a modern head waiter (originally he was the person who tested the food given to the king)

divers various

1 **If it were done** if the murder were finished and done with

3 **trammel** catch together (like a net)

4 **with his surcease success** what I want (success) by his death

5 **the be-all and the end-all** death all that is to be and what completes everything

6 **bank and shoal** life like a sand bank in the sea of eternity

7 **jump ... come** risk the judgement of the after life

8 **still** always

10 **even-handed** impartial

11 **Commends** offers

ingredience contents

chalice drinking vessel (particularly in the Christian communion service)

14 **Strong both** both strong arguments

17 **faculties** powers (as king)

18 **clear** incorrupt

20 **taking-off** departure, murder

21 **naked new-born babe** suggests compassion for the innocent and helpless

22 **Striding the blast** astride the storm (of protest)

cherubin angel

23 **sightless curriers** invisible winds

24 **blow** broadcast (or trumpet)

25 **tears ... wind** tears of pity shall outdo the wind of indignation

25–6 **spur ... sides** powerful or moral incentive to urge him, just like a horse approaching a jump, into the act of murder

27 **Vaulting** soaring, aspiring

27–8 **o'erleaps ... other** jumps beyond its control and comes to grief over the jump

32 **bought** gained (by his deeds)

34 **would** should

newest gloss new and shining

37 **green and pale** the effects of being drunk

39 **Such** as drunken boasting

42 **ornament of life** the crown

45 **poor cat i'the adage** the cat in the proverb wanted to eat a fish but was not prepared to wet his feet in order to catch it

Prithee, peace I pray you, stop speaking

47 **none** not a man

48 **break this enterprise** voice this plan

52 **Did then adhere** were convenient then

53 **fitness** suitability (of time and place)

60 **screw ... sticking place** tighten your courage like the string holding the arrow in a cross-bow which is ready for shooting

62 **the rather** certainly

63 **chamberlains** personal servants

64 **wassail** feasting

convince overpower

65-7 **memory ... limbeck only** memory, the guardian of reason, will be converted into a vapour (by alcohol) and the brain act as a distilling unit

68 **drenchèd** drunken

71 **spongy** filled with drink

72 **quell** murder

73 **mettle** spirit

74 **received** believed

79 **bend ... agent** strain (like a bow-string) every part of my being

81 **mock the time** deceive everyone

ACT II

SCENE 1

It is after midnight and Banquo and Fleance, his son, are preparing to go to bed. Banquo feels some uneasiness but when Macbeth appears suddenly out of the darkness he converses politely and passes on Duncan's compliments to Macbeth and a diamond for Lady Macbeth. Macbeth advises Banquo to side with him in the future. Left on his own,

Macbeth waits for the signal from his wife; his imagination conjures out of the air a dagger which he cannot grasp. He prepares his mind for the murder and the signal sounds.

Immediately before the murder we are presented with Banquo and Macbeth who have both gained military glory, promising prophecies from the Witches, and praise from the king. It would seem from lines 7–9 and line 20 that the meeting with the Witches has made a lasting impression on Banquo's mind and he is deeply disturbed by the workings of his subconscious mind in dreams. His trust rests on God and the help of his angels. Macbeth too has an imaginative flight in the scene but in his **soliloquy** he allies himself with witchcraft, murder and secrecy. The contrast with Banquo is carefully offered at this point. The 'summons' to sleep that Banquo feels in line 6 has become a summons 'to heaven or to hell' for Duncan, according to Macbeth in the final line of the scene.

4 **husbandry** economy

5 **Their candles** the stars of heaven

6 **summons** tiredness which calls him

7 **powers** the order of angels who protect man from devils

14 **largess** generous gifts

offices servants

16–17 **shut up ... content** gone to bed completely happy

18–19 **Our will ... wrought** we were not able to be as hospitable as we should have wished

22 **entreat ... to serve** find the time

24 **your kind'st leisure** your convenience

25 **cleave ... when 'tis** side with me when the time comes

26 **honour ... none** Macbeth seems to mean gain; Banquo means honesty

28 **bosom ... clear** heart free from guilt and loyalty unspoilt

36–7 **sensible To feeling** able to be touched

39 **heat-oppressèd** fevered

40 **palpable** able to be touched

42 **marshall'st** indicate

46 **dudgeon** handle

gouts drops

48 **informs** creates shapes

49 **half-world** hemisphere

50 **abuse** deceive

52 **Hecat** goddess of witchcraft

offerings ceremonies, rituals

53 **Alarumed** aroused

54 **watch** indication of time

55 **Tarquin's ravishing strides** Tarquin raped Lucretia in the night (see Shakespeare's poem *The Rape of Lucrece*)

58 **prate** tell

59 **take ... the time** broadcast the horror beyond this time

63 **knell** bell sounded to announce a death

SCENE 2

Lady Macbeth has drugged Duncan's servants and now, stimulated by wine, she awaits the completion of the murder and the return of her husband. Macbeth enters, almost out of his mind, unable to distance himself from the scene in Duncan's room. He is rebuked by his wife who, seizing control of the situation, finds that she has to take the daggers back because Macbeth has removed them and is incapable of returning to the scene of his crime. A sound of knocking is heard and Macbeth is led out by his wife to wash off the blood and change into his dressing gown.

A scene of intense excitement where the suspense worked up by Lady Macbeth's vivid recounting of her preparations is heightened by her jumpiness and is not in any way relieved by the return of Macbeth with the news, 'I have done the deed'. Macbeth's state of mind verges on the hysterical and the extreme tension is communicated to us so that we are forced to participate in it by the abrupt changes of direction in the speech of the characters, the interruptions, the sudden noises, the questions, the exclamations. We are trapped in Macbeth's anguish and, like Lady Macbeth, we struggle for control. We see the bloody daggers in Macbeth's hands and, like the characters, we come to fear discovery – such is our involvement, our complicity in the murder. We feel that *we* cannot go back with the daggers, and, when the knocking repeatedly sounds, *we* are held in the hysteria of Macbeth and are grateful to be led off by the masterful Lady Macbeth.

SCENE 2 continued

2 **quenched** put them out (to sleep)
3 **owl** bird associated with death (as are crickets in line 15)
   fatal bellman the man who rings the bell announcing the execution of a
   condemned criminal
4 **stern'st** most solemn
5 **surfeited grooms** drunken servants
6 **charge** duty
   possets bed-time drinks
24 **addressed** prepared
27 **hangman** executioner
37 **knits ... sleave** arranges the tangled threads
39 **second course** the most nourishing course of a meal
45 **unbend** loosen
47 **witness** evidence
52 **Infirm** weak
54 **as pictures** look the same
56–7 **gild ... guilt** cover with golden blood (a play on words)
58 **how is't** what is wrong
60 **Neptune** Roman god of the sea
61 **rather** instead
62 **multitudinous** extensive
   incarnadine turn red
63 **one** totally
68–9 **Your ... unattended** your firmness of mind has deserted you
71 **watchers** awake
72 **poorly** helplessly

SCENE 3

As the knocking increases the Porter, still drunk, organises himself to
open the gate and, eventually, he lets Macduff and Lennox enter.
Macbeth appears, apparently wakened by the noise. When Macduff, who
has gone to waken the king, returns with the news of his murder and
raises the alarm, Macbeth and Lennox go to investigate. Lady Macbeth
enters followed by Banquo and, while the news is discussed, Macbeth
relates how he killed the blood-covered servants in his fury. Lady
Macbeth faints and in the ensuing confusion Malcolm and Donalbain

decide to slip away because they fear for their lives. Banquo proposes a general meeting to discuss the situation and the others agree.

The tension of the previous scene is maintained by the knocking and by our feeling that the discovery of the murder is merely being delayed by the rambling talk. The horror of the murder is intensified by the coarse vulgarity of the Porter; it seems, in his comic bad taste, to be a gruesome attempt to cover up the truth. He does, however, when we examine his words more carefully, give a contemporary and a universal significance to Macbeth's crime. Lennox's observations develop this wider significance. Also, the confused quality of the Porter's speech and our uncertainty as to what is happening suggest a general confusion which, in fact, occupies the rest of the scene. Macbeth and Lady Macbeth's actions and words are a mixture of the extravagant and plausible. It is interesting to compare Macbeth's words in lines 88–93 with his speech in V.5.17–28. Banquo, more than Macbeth, proves himself the master of the situation and his speech near the end of the scene is judicious, firm and clear-spoken. The flight of Malcolm and Donalbain is an intimation of the distrust and moral confusion soon to be seen as characteristic of Macbeth's behaviour as king.

2 **old** plenty (of work)

4 **Dolaobub** the devil

5 **Come in time (time-server** in some editions) come in good time (or come in, you opportunist)

 napkins enow plenty of handkerchiefs

8 **equivocator** one who tampers with the truth to suit his argument (The Catholic Jesuits involved in the plot against King James in 1605 were notorious for their equivocations.)

13 **stealing ... hose** cheating by using less material in the trousers than he claimed

14 **roast your goose** heat your tailor's iron (or it may mean cure your venereal disease)

18 **primrose ... bonfire** the seductive, pleasurable way to hell

22-3 **second cock** three o'clock in the morning

23 **provoker** encourager

27–33 **Lechery ... leaves him** the Porter is claiming here that alcohol arouses a man sexually but weakens his ability at the same time

34 **gave ... the lie** knocked you down

38 **made a shift** managed

    cast throw him off, vomit

43 **timely** early

47 **physics** counteracts

49 **limited** appointed

    service duty

55 **dire combustion** impending disasters

56 **to the woeful time** for the time of distress

    obscure bird owl

63 **Confusion** destruction

65 **The Lord's anointed temple** the body and the king

69 **Gorgon** anyone who looked at this mythical monster was turned to stone

73 **downy** gentle

    counterfeit imitation

75 **The Great Doom's image** a picture of the Final Judgement Day

77 **countenance** face

90 **serious** worthwhile

92 **lees** dregs of wine

93 **vault** wine cellar, the arch of the sky

94 **amiss** wrong

99 **badged** marked

107 **expedition** haste

108 **pauser** what should make one hesitate

109 **laced** criss-crossed

111 **wasteful** destructive

113 **Unmannerly breeched** disgustingly covered

117 **That most ... for ours** who are most involved in this business

119 **auger-hole** a tiny, unsuspected hole

120 **brewed** matured

121 **upon the foot of motion** able to do anything

123 **naked frailties** underclad bodies (but this also implies human feelings)

126 **scruples** doubts

128 **undivulged pretence** unrevealed aims

130 **manly readiness** suitable clothes (or prepared as men)

132 **consort** gather

133 **office** duty

137 **the nea'er** the nearer

138 **shaft** arrow

139 **lighted** landed finally

140 **aim** man who aims

141 **dainty** particular

142-3 **There's ... steals itself** it is justified (theft) to steal away

SCENE 4

Ross and an Old Man discuss the extraordinary confusion in the natural world and draw a parallel between it and the unnatural human acts of the night. Macduff enters and reports that suspicion for the responsibility of the murder rests on the departed Malcolm and Donalbain. Macbeth has gone to be crowned in Scone.

> We receive a view of the incident from people not directly concerned in it. The Old Man, significantly given the biblical span of life, is representative of the common man and the murder of Duncan is made more horrific by its uniqueness in his experience. The turbulence in the macrocosm, the reversals of natural law, reflect the enormity of Macbeth's crime. The second half of the scene is mainly an informative link between the murder and subsequent developments in the play but the scene ends with a human and Christian hope that the traditional values will be restored.

4 **trifled former knowings** made earlier experience seem trifling

6-7 **heavens ... act ... stage** all these words have a theatrical sense

8 **travelling lamp** sun

9 **predominance** supremacy (of the power of darkness)

11 **towering ... place** soaring to the highest point of her flight

12 **mousing** (usually content to) hunt mice

15 **minions** darlings, best

16 **flung out** lashed out

24 **pretend** hope for

   suborned paid to commit a crime

28 **Thriftless** wasteful

    raven up ravenously devour
29 **means** support, basis
31 **named** chosen
    Scone place where Scottish kings were crowned
32 **invested** crowned as king
33 **Colmekill** Iona, a holy island, where Scottish kings were buried
36 **Fife** Macduff's territory
37 **Adieu** (French for) good-bye
38 **Lest ... new** it may be that the new regime will be less comfortable to us
40 **benison** blessing
41 **good ... foes** see the best in people (a reference to the peacemakers of the Bible)

ACT III

SCENE 1

Macbeth has settled into the Royal Palace at Forres. Banquo has serious suspicions about how the Witches' prophecies for Macbeth have been fulfilled but he and, it turns out, Macbeth, remember the Witches' prediction for his descendants. Publicly, Banquo and Macbeth are polite and diplomatic but when Banquo leaves to go riding, Macbeth, aware of the threat posed by Banquo's qualities, arranges for his murder and the murder of Fleance by two villains whose minds he turns against Banquo.

We see Macbeth in this scene as the established king but his mind is not secure. We hear Banquo's thoughts of Macbeth before we hear the king's own thoughts and Shakespeare has arranged the thoughts in parallel so that they refer forward and back to each other. But Banquo says nothing of Macbeth's qualities as a king or even as a man, whereas Macbeth presents a generous analysis of Banquo's character. Both men seem to be obsessed by the predictions of the Witches concerning the descendants of Banquo. Macbeth, however, thinks that he can negate the prediction by killing Banquo and Fleance, even though the same prophets have been proved correct in his own case. Notice the casual skill with which Macbeth ascertains Banquo's movements, and the care he takes, so as to avoid any suspicion, to mention repeatedly the importance he places on Banquo's presence at the special supper in the evening and at the meeting the following day. It seems curious that Shakespeare devotes so much time, about seventy lines, to Macbeth's meeting with the two Murderers. The sorting-out and manipulation of other people are marks of the tyrant. 'To be thus is nothing; / But to be safely thus' (lines 47–8), he says while waiting for the Murderers, and his elaborate briefing of them is an attempt to persuade himself of how foolproof his plan is. He, paradoxically, appeals to them as men.

4 **stand ... posterity** continue in your family

s.d. **Sennet** a set of notes played on the trumpet

13 **all-thing** totally

14 **solemn** ceremonious

21 **still** always

    grave and prosperous weighty and profitable

32 **invention** lies

34 **Craving us jointly** demanding us both

36 **our time ... upon's** it is time for us to go

44 **While** till

47 **thus** king

50 **would** must

51 **dauntless temper** fearless quality

55 **genius is rebuked** guardian spirit is held down

56 **chid** challenged

61 **sceptre** the symbol of the king

62 **unlineal** outside my family

64 **issue** descendants

    filed defiled, corrupted

66 **rancours ... peace** bitterness in my calm of mind

67 **eternal jewel** soul

68 **enemy** Devil

70 **list** struggle (tournament)

71 **champion ... utterance** fight me to the death

78 **made good** explained

79 **passed in probation** showed the proof

80 **borne in hand** deceived

    crossed tricked

82 **half ... crazed** a simpleton

87 **so gospelled** such Christians

90 **yours** your families

92–3 **hounds, etc** different breeds of dogs

93 **clept** called

94 **valued file** list showing the qualities and value

99 **Particular addition** individual description (unlike the bill and catalogue)

101–2 **file ... rank** the positions of men in an army; file suggests more quality

105 **Grapples** holds you tight

106 **his** Banquo's

111 **tugged with** pulled about by

115 **in such bloody distance** of such a fatal closeness

117 **near'st of life** very being

119 **avouch** justify

120 **For** because of

121 **wail** must lament

125 **sundry** various

129 **perfect spy** exact information

131 **something** some distance

    thought bearing in mind

132 **clearness** clean reputation

133 **rubs nor botches** flaws or mistakes

135 **material** important

136 **embrace** share

137 **Resolve** make your plan

139 **straight** immediately

SCENE 2

Lady Macbeth realises that the satisfaction she and Macbeth had sought has not been achieved. She tries to enter into her husband's obsessive involvement while, at the same time, trying to reassure him and urge him to cheerfulness. Macbeth is tormented, his thoughts are fixed on Banquo. He hints at black deeds to come.

    A pathetic development in the relationship of Macbeth and Lady Macbeth is revealed. They feel similarly about the situation

(compare lines 4–7 and 19–22) but are unable to share their
thoughts with each other and, by now, Macbeth has detached
himself from his reliance on his wife and pursues his own course. It
is remarkable that in the middle of this scene he can ask his wife to
act pleasantly to Banquo when we know that Banquo, on his orders,
will never return. His brutalised nature is evident in the cool 'Be
innocent of the knowledge, dearest chuck, / Till thou applaud the
deed.' Significantly, he invokes the same powers of darkness and
witchcraft as he had called on earlier in II.1.51–60.

4 **had** gained
7 **doubtful** apprehensive, insecure
9 **sorriest** most miserable
10 **Using** as companions
12 **without regard** out of thought
13 **scorched** slashed
14 **close** recover
   poor malice weak attack
15 **former tooth** still poisonous fangs
16 **frame ... disjoint** the whole universe break apart
   both ... worlds heaven and earth
17 **Ere** before
22 **ecstasy** delirium
23 **fitful** restless
25 **levy** troops
27 **sleek o'er** smooth
28 **jovial** foster good humour
30 **remembrance** reminder
31 **Present him eminence** honour him
32–3 **Unsafe ... streams** while we are unsafe we must give a clean look to our
   honour by using streams of flattery
34 **vizards** masks
38 **nature's ... eterne** they are made in God's image but are not immortal
40 **jocund** joyful
41 **cloistered** round cloisters of churches, or dark
42 **shard-born** born in dung, or carried on its scaly wings
43 **yawning peal** call to sleep

44 **note** significance
45 **chuck** chick (term of endearment)
46 **seeling** blinding (as is done to a hawk's eyelids)
47 **Scarf** blindfold
49 **bond** the moral (biblical) law which forbids killing
50 **pale** anxious
   thickens dims
51 **rooky** full of rooks
54 **ill** evil, worse

SCENE 3

Some distance from the Palace, a third Murderer, sent by Macbeth, joins the two waiting to ambush Banquo and Fleance. In the gathering darkness they kill Banquo but Fleance escapes.

Macbeth cannot trust the two Murderers and sends one of his men to make sure the job is done. When Fleance escapes, Macbeth's scheme has more than failed; he has increased suspicions of his villainy, and the prophecy of the Witches, which he had hoped to cancel, is still there to torment him. Banquo himself was not the real danger and Macbeth's already overwhelmed conscience is further pressed under the weight of a murder he knows to be indefensible.

2 **He ... mistrust** there is no reason for us to distrust him (the newcomer)
3 **offices** instructions
4 **To ... just** just as we were directed
6 **lated** belated
   apace quickly
7 **timely** welcome
10 **within ... expectation** on the list of expected guests
11 **about** the long way round (to the stables)
19 **way** right thing to do
21 **Best ... affair** the more important part of the job, or the larger part of the reward

SCENE 4

As Macbeth and Lady Macbeth are welcoming the guests to the feast,
one of the Murderers arrives and tells Macbeth of the death of Banquo
and the escape of Fleance. Macbeth turns back to the table and
comments on Banquo's absence. Banquo's ghost enters and occupies
Macbeth's place; he is visible only to Macbeth. Lady Macbeth tries to
calm her husband and keep control of the situation but after the ghost has
disappeared and Macbeth seems to be recovering, suddenly, again on
Macbeth's mentioning his name, Banquo's ghost reappears and Macbeth
is rendered helpless. After the ghost has gone for the second time, Lady
Macbeth brings the feast to a hurried end. Macbeth informs Lady
Macbeth that he intends to visit the Witches and press on with
eliminating all opposition.

This, the halfway scene in the play, is a central scene in the
analysis of Macbeth's career in crime. The newly established
king holds a lavish feast to show his authority and at the beginning
of the scene we have the ceremony of guests and hosts and civilised
order interrupted by the sly appearance of Macbeth's hired
killer. The facade of decency has a murderous heart and the
appearance of Banquo's ghost is the harsh reminder of Macbeth's
wickedness. The ghost is the externalised form of Macbeth's guilt
and fear of discovery, invisible to the others but a terrifying reality
to Macbeth himself. His wife loyally and resourcefully tries to
protect him and shake him out of his obsession but, as she says,
Macbeth is 'quite unmanned in folly'. Macbeth, a man celebrated
for his courage in battle, cringes before the creation of his
troubled conscience. When the ghost and the guests have gone,
Macbeth's mind is not restored to calmness or repentance or even
full trust in his wife. He can see no way out of his dilemma but by
crushing everyone around him who questions his will. Fate,
including the Witches, must be bullied into obedience. This is the
final appearance of a sane Lady Macbeth. Her iron self-control,
loyalty to her husband, organising skill, apparent callousness – all
evident in this scene – are qualities she possesses but, as we shall see,
she has paid dearly for them.

1 **degrees** places at table (according to importance)

1–2 **At first And last** from beginning to end

5 **state** special chair of state

　　in best at the most suitable

6 **require** request

9 **encounter** answer

10 **sides** sides of the table

11 **Be large in mirth** enjoy yourselves

18 **the nonpareil** without equal

21 **Whole** solid

　　founded secure

22 **broad and general** free and unconfined

　　casing surrounding

23 **cabined, etc.** imprisoned

24 **saucy** molesting

26 **trenchèd** cut deep

28 **worm** young serpent

31 **ourselves** each other

32 **cheer** welcome, or a toast

32–6 **The feast ... without it** unless repeated welcomes are given, a feast is like a paid-for meal; food itself is better at home but outside one expects more ceremony to make the meal worthwhile

39 **honour roofed** all the nobility present

40 **graced** gracious

42 **mischance** misfortune

47 **moves** disturbs

50 **gory locks** blood-covered hair

54 **upon a thought** in a moment

55 **note** make a fuss

56 **passion** fit

59 **proper stuff!** nonsense

62 **flaws** outbursts

65 **grandam** grandmother

70–3 **If charnel houses ... kites** if tombs cannot hold down the dead we will need to have them eaten by birds of prey

75 **purged ... weal** civilised society

80 **mortal murders** fatal wounds

80 **crowns** heads

83 **lack** miss

90 **thirst** wish to drink

91 **all to all** everyone toast everyone

duties homage

pledge the toast

92 **Avaunt!** away!

94 **speculation** intelligence

100 **Hyrcan** place near the Caspian Sea

104 **inhabit** have in me

protest accuse

105 **baby** doll

109 **admired** amazing

110 **overcome** come over

111–12 **strange ... owe** wonder about my own nature

118 **order** order of rank

121 **It will have** murder demands

123 **Augurs** prophecies

relations connections in nature

124 **maggot-pies, etc** types of birds

125 **man of blood** murderer

127 **How say'st thou** what do you say to the fact

denies his person refuses his presence

131 **fee'd** bribed

132 **betimes** very early

133 **bent** determined

135 **causes** considerations

139 **may be scanned** can be examined

140 **season** preservative, or freshening

141–2 **My ... use** my strange delusion is the result of a beginner's fear, one who needs more experience

143 **deed** crimes

SCENE 5

On the heath, Hecat, the ruler of all witches, is angry that she has not been consulted about the previous dealings with Macbeth. She tells the

Witches to prepare for a meeting with him in the morning and she predicts his downfall.

Many scholars doubt whether this scene was written by Shakespeare but in its **imagery** and attitude to Macbeth it fits easily into the rest of the play. The wild determination obvious in Macbeth at the end of Scene 4 is remarked on by Hecat.

2 **beldams** hags

3 **Saucy** impudent

7 **close contriver** secret inventor

11 **wayward son** not a member of their circle

15 **Acheron** hell

21 **Unto a dismal** preparing for a disastrous
   end purpose

24 **profound** heavy

26 **sleights** arts

30 **spurn** ignore

32 **security** a sense of false security

scene 6

Lennox examines the recent 'accidents' and the evidence points to Macbeth's involvement. Macbeth has sent a rebuke to Macduff for his absence at the feast but Macduff has gone to England to rouse support against Macbeth. The opposition to Macbeth is growing.

Although this scene follows immediately on the previous one, we are given a sense of a stretch of time and, just as at the end of Act II, a larger perspective on events. The sense of Macbeth's tyranny, like a modern police state, is communicated very acutely in Lennox's analysis of events. He is ironic, oblique and somewhat guarded even if the implication of his remarks is quite clear. Macbeth is trying to tighten his hold on the country but the opposition is difficult to pin down and the English King, 'most pious Edward', is obviously prepared to help against Macbeth. Some intimation of Macduff's approaching tragedy is given in the final lines which connect with what Macbeth hinted at in the final lines of Scene 4.

1 **hit** agreed with
2 **Which ... further** and you can draw your own conclusions
3 **borne** arranged
4 **marry** by Mary
8 **want the thought** fail to think
11 **delinquents** criminals
12 **thralls** slaves
20 **'twere** it were worth
21 **broad** frank
    failed declined
25 **due of birth** the throne
28 **malevolence ... respect** his misfortunes lessen the high honour given to him
30 **upon aid** to help him
31 **Northumberland** on the Scottish border
33 **ratify** sanction
36 **faithful** honest
    free with no conditions attached
41 **cloudy** frowning
42 **rue** regret
43 **clogs** burdens
44 **to a caution** to take care

ACT IV

SCENE 1

The Witches prepare a foul concoction and arrange their spell. When Macbeth enters they agree to answer his enquiries and three Apparitions appear in order: an armed head, who warns Macbeth against Macduff; a bloody child who tells him that he cannot be harmed by one 'born of woman'; and a crowned child carrying a tree who guarantees Macbeth's safety until Birnan Wood comes to Dunsinane Hill. In answer to his question concerning Banquo's descendants, Macbeth is shown eight Kings ushered in by the spirit of Banquo. The Witches disappear and Lennox arrives with the news of Macduff's flight to England. Macbeth decides to kill every member of Macduff's family.

The Witches' broth is made as unpleasant and un-Christian as possible to prepare the audience's minds for the arrival of Macbeth

and to offer some parallel to the wickedness practised by Macbeth.
Macbeth addresses the Witches almost familiarly and he 'conjures'
them in their own manner. The Apparitions are obviously symbolic.
The most straightforward interpretation sees the figures as (1)
prophetic of the killed Macbeth, (2) the infant Macduff, and (3)
young Malcolm coming to Dunsinane. Macbeth, typically, wishes
to accept the favourable predictions and reject what is awkward for
him, and his horror at Banquo's ghost has much to do with his
sense of powerlessness to prevent Banquo's family eventually
succeeding to the throne. His impotent rage expresses itself in the
pointless plan to massacre Macduff's family. As was noticeable in
Act III Scene 5, the Witches are using Macbeth for their own
purposes and Macbeth proves himself adaptable material even if in
his better judgement he knows them to be evil and unreliable. The
flight of Macduff seems to confirm their prophecies.

1 **brinded** streaky coloured

2 **hedge-pig** hedgehog

3 **Harpier** spirit of the witch

8 **Sweltered venom** sweated poison

12 **fenny** slimy (from the marshes)

16 **fork** forked tongue

17 **howlet** owl

23 **mummy** preserved body

    maw and gulf belly and gullet

25 **hemlock** poisonous plant

26, 29 **Jew, Turk, Tartar** non-Christians

27 **yew** grown in churchyards

28 **eclipse** associated with catastrophes

31 **Ditch-delivered** born in a ditch

    drab prostitute

32 **slab** slimy

33 **chaudron** entrails

44 **pricking** omen of approaching evil

52 **yesty** foaming

54 **lodged** beaten down

58 **germens** seeds

59 **sicken** be sick with its own work

64 **farrow** young pigs

65 **gibbet** the tree where the murderer is hanged

67 **office** your works

73 **harped** guessed

83 **take a bond of fate** guarantee the promise of fate by killing Macduff

87–8 **round And top** crown

90 **chafes** protests

92 **Birnan ... Dunsinane** places separated by ten miles

94 **impress** conscript

95 **bodements** prophecies

96 **Rebellious** against him and death, compare III.4.70–2

98 **lease of nature** his natural lifetime

99 **mortal custom** natural death

s.d. ***eight kings*** the Stuart line leading to James I

112 **sear** burn

116 **crack of doom** the Last Day

118 **glass** mirror

120 **two-fold ... sceptres** symbols to show that they rule over England, Scotland and Ireland

122 **boltered** matted

129 **antic** fantastic

144 **flighty** fleeting

145 **deed go with it** we act immediately

146 **firstlings** first impulses

152 **trace** follow

154 **sights** apparitions

SCENE 2

In Macduff's castle in Fife, Ross tries to explain to Lady Macduff why her husband has hurried off to England. She finds his desertion of his family impossible to justify. A stranger arrives as she is discussing the situation with her son, warns her to escape immediately, but he has barely departed when Macbeth's murderers break in and kill her and her son.

This scene has the moving quality of a particular family atrocity. Lady Macduff and her son are presented to us as pathetically vulnerable. The futility of Lady Macduff's condemnation of her husband's unexplained departure heightens our sense of her political innocence. Ross and the Messenger, fresh from the Court of Macbeth, know how tyranny operates and how the individual has to act secretly to survive. The glib cleverness of her young son has the same pathos. We know that Macbeth's agents are on their way and the discussion between mother and son is wasted breath.

4 **make us traitors** make us look like traitors

7 **titles** property

9 **wants ... touch** lacks ordinary affection

10 **will fight** will fight for

14 **cuz** form of 'cousin'

15 **school** control

17 **fits o' the season** uncertainties of the time

19–20 **hold rumour From** believe rumours inspired by

24–5 **Things ... before** he says that the situation can only improve

129 **disgrace** shame (because he would weep)

36 **net ... gin** traps to catch birds

43 **wit** cleverness

48 **swears and lies** swears an oath (promise) and then breaks it

57 **enow** enough

64 **prattler** chatterer

66 **your state ... perfect** I certainly know your noble rank

67 **doubt** suspect

68 **homely** humble

71 **do worse** not to warn you

    fell savage

72 **Which** the cruelty

76 **laudable** praiseworthy

81 **unsanctified** unprotected

84 **fry** offspring

SCENE 3

In the King of England's palace, Macduff describes the horrors of Macbeth's reign. Malcolm queries Macduff's political integrity and, when Macduff urges that Macbeth must be deposed, he presents a picture of himself as worse even than Macbeth. Macduff shows his honesty by rejecting the idea of such a king and Malcolm admits that he has been testing Macduff's loyalty to Scotland and declares himself ready to lead an attack on Macbeth. The King of England is treating sick subjects and as Malcolm describes the cure to Macduff, Ross arrives with news of the slaughter of the Macduff family. After Macduff has expressed his grief it is agreed that the time has arrived for the attack on Macbeth.

> This scene is longer and slower-moving than any other in the play. The main function of the scene is to assemble and assess the moral forces present in the drama before the final attack on Macbeth's corruption is launched. Malcolm, the murdered Duncan's son and claimant to the throne, and Macduff, who remained with Macbeth but has led the internal opposition to him; these two are appropriate characters to review the situation in Scotland and look forward to the possibility of a brighter future. The attack on evil must come when the forces of goodness are mobilised *and* the emotional intensity is right. The army is ready but the news of the brutal slaughter of Macduff's family signals the right moment.

3 **mortal** deadly

4 **Bestride ... birthdom** defend our fallen native land

8 **Like ... dolour** the same cry of sorrow

10 **to friend** propitious, convenient

12 **sole** very

15 **deserve ... me** gain from him by using me

     and wisdom and it may be wise

19–20 **recoil ... charge** do something wicked if ordered to by the king

21 **transpose** alter

22 **brightest** Satan

26 **rawness** helpless condition

27 **motives** influences

29 **jealousies** suspicions

30 **rightly just** completely honest

33 **check** cross-examine

34 **affeered** confirmed

37 **to boot** in addition

38 **fear** doubt

41 **withal** moreover

43 **England** the king

51 **grafted** planted

55 **confineless harms** boundless evils

57 **top** surpass

58 **Luxurious** · lustful

59 **Sudden** violent

61 **voluptuousness** lechery

64 **continent** restraining

71 **Convey** indulge secretly

72 **time ... hoodwink** may deceive the people

74–6 **to devour ... inclined** many will offer themselves to the king

77 **ill-composed affection** wicked nature

78 **staunchless** limitless

82 **forge** invent

86 **summer-seeming** short-lived

88 **foisons** plenty

89 **Of ... own** in your own possession

portable tolerable

96 **division** variations

several different

98 **Uproar** destroy

104 **untitled** illegal

107 **interdiction** condemnation

108 **blaspheme ... breed** slander his parents

111 **Died** prepared for death

114 **Thy** the hope of his heart

118 **trains** tricks

119 **modest ... me** ordinary caution pulls me back

123 **Unspeak** cancel

abjure reject

126 **forsworn** dishonest

135 **at a point** prepared

136 **goodness** success

137 **Be like ... quarrel** equal the justness of our cause

142 **stay** await

convinces is beyond
143 **assay of art** medical skill
145 **presently** immediately
146 **Evil** scrofula
148 **here-remain** stay
149 **solicits** persuades
150 **strangely visited** curiously afflicted
152 **mere** very
153 **stamp** coin
155 **leaves** hands down
156 **benediction** power, blessing
    virtue power
159 **speak** proclaim
162 **betimes** quickly
169 **marked** noticed
170 **modern ecstasy** commonplace emotion
173 **or ... sicken** before they have time to fall ill
174 **nice** elaborate
175 **doth ... speaker** causes the teller to be booed
176 **teems** is born
180 **niggard** miser
183 **out** in rebellion
184 **witnessed** evidenced
188 **doff** remove
192 **gives out** can provide
195 **latch** catch
196 **fee-grief** individual sorrow
202 **possess** inform
204 **surprised** attacked suddenly
206 **quarry** dead bodies
210 **Whispers ... heart** whispers to the overburdened heart
217 **hell-kite** bird of prey from hell
218 **dam** mother
    fell savage
219 **Dispute** struggle against
224 **Naught** wicked
225 **demerits** sins

ACT IV, SCENE 3 continued

226 **whetstone** sharpener

229 **play ... eyes** weep

231 **intermission** delay

234 **too** and me

235–6 **our ... leave** we need only take our leave

238 **Put ... instruments** urge on their human agents

ACT V

SCENE 1

In Dunsinane Castle a doctor and Lady Macbeth's lady-in-waiting are watching to see if Lady Macbeth walks in her sleep as her servant has reported to the doctor. She enters and begins to rub her hands as if struggling to clean them and before she departs she refers to the deaths of Duncan, Macduff's wife and Banquo. The doctor confesses that he is incapable of dealing with such cases.

> We have not seen Lady Macbeth since Act III Scene 4 and her behaviour in the present scene shows that her carefully contrived mask has slipped. In her sleep-walking she reveals the guilts and anxieties by which she is tortured. Particularly, she re-enacts the first murder scene when she took the initiative and organised a stumbling Macbeth. Now, alone, her loyalty to her husband remains intact; only once does she reproach him, 'no more o' that. You mar all with this starting'. Her behaviour is revealing and also very moving. She has given all and now her present is overwhelmed by the past. 'What's done cannot be undone'. A candle is no protection against murky hell.

4 **field** fighting

6 **closet** chest

9 **perturbation** upset

10 **effects of watching** actions of one awake

16 **meet** appropriate

19 **Lo** look

     guise habit

20 **close** hidden

42 **mar ... starting** spoil everything with your nervousness

50 **sorely charged** heavily burdened

52 **dignity** worth

55 **practice** knowledge

67 **abroad** about

72 **annoyance** injury

74 **mated** bewildered

SCENE 2

Scottish rebel forces prepare to join with Malcolm's English army near
Birnan Wood. Reports suggest that Macbeth is becoming more desperate
and his support is deserting him.

A series of short scenes gives the impression of swift action and
manoeuvring armies. Macbeth is being gradually isolated. Even his
wife has been shown to have collapsed under the pressure and, as
the besieging force strengthens, Macbeth is left more and more on
his own. The description of him is parallel to the picture of his wife
in the previous scene.

s.d. **colours** banners

1 **power** army

3 **dear** heartfelt

4 **bleeding** bloody

alarm call to battle

5 **Excite** rouse

mortified dead

8 **file** list

10 **unrough** beardless

11 **Protest ... manhood** want to show they are grown up

15 **buckle ... cause** keep control of his disorderly forces

18 **minutely** minute by minute

upbraid rebuke

faith-breach treachery

19 **in** because of

23 **pestered senses** tormented nerves

27 **sickly weal** diseased country

28 **purge** cleansing

30 **dew** nourish
sovereign flower King Malcolm

SCENE 3

Macbeth, besieged in Dunsinane Castle, puts a desperate trust in the
Witches' predictions. He has become violent and inconsistent with his
servants, despairing in himself. The doctor's diagnosis of Lady Macbeth's
condition gives Macbeth no comfort but he asks the doctor to find a
remedy for Scotland's situation.

Macbeth's conduct and speech have become wild. He repeats
himself, contradicts himself and does not seem able to listen
properly to what others say. When the doctor tells him about Lady
Macbeth, Macbeth seems more concerned to shout at the doctor
and demand a cure for his own situation than with a treatment for
his wife. But behind the shouting, Macbeth realises that he is
coming to the end of his resources, nobody is freely loyal to him and
his shouting prevents him from considering his situation calmly and
realistically.

1 **them** the thanes
3 **taint** be infected
5 **consequences** developments
8 **epicures** luxury lovers
9 **sway** am moved
11 **black** at the time of the play the damned in hell were thought to be black
loon foolish boy
12 **goose** cowardly and stupid
14 **prick ... fear** make your face red by pinching it in order to hide your fear
15 **lily-livered** cowardly
patch fool
16 **linen** white of cowardice
17 **counsellors** encouragers
whey-face milk-white face
20 **push** crisis
21 **chair** establish
dis-seat unthrone

22 **way** course

23 **sere** withered condition

yellow of autumn and dying

27 **mouth-honour** lip-service

28 **fain** like to

35 **skirr** scour

38 **thick-coming** recurring

40 **minister to** treat

42 **Raze out** erase

43 **oblivious antidote** cure that makes one forget

47 **physic** medical skill

48 **staff** spear

50 **dispatch** hurry

50-1 **cast ... land** analyse the urine (of Scotland)

52 **pristine** fresh

54 **Pull't off** pull off his armour

55 **rhubarb, senna** purgative plants

56 **scour** cleanse

58 **it** (some piece of his armour)

59 **bane** harm

62 **Profit** money

SCENE 4

The army assembled against Macbeth is ordered by Malcolm to cut branches from Birnan Wood to disguise the number of soldiers. They march confidently towards Dunsinane.

The Witches' promise in which Macbeth put such trust is revealed as open to different meanings. The quiet confidence and the professionalism apparent in Malcolm's army are in sharp contrast to the shouting, boasting and disorganisation shown by Macbeth in the previous scene. All the Scottish nobles who have appeared earlier in the play are now allied against Macbeth.

2 **chambers** bedrooms

5 **shadow** conceal

6 **discovery** spies

7 **Err** mistake (our numbers)

9 **endure** not prevent

10 **Our ... before't** us besieging it

11 **advantage to be given** opportunity to escape presents itself

12 **more and less** great and small

15 **Attend ... event** await the outcome

17 **due decision** certainty

18 **owe** actually possess

20 **certain ... arbitrate** fighting must decide the actual result

SCENE 5

In the castle Macbeth is preparing to withstand the siege when he is told of his wife's death. As the emptiness of his life is brought home to him a messenger arrives with the news that Birnam Wood is approaching Dunsinane. He realises that all is lost but decides to die fighting.

It is possible that Macbeth's castle could withstand a long siege but there is a mixture of boasting, detachment from ordinary life and loss in his claim that he is now unmoved by fear. Lady Macbeth's death, possibly by her own hand, reduces his bravado and resolution to empty words. Life seems futile and deceptive (compare his false words in II.3.88–93). The report of Birnan Wood's movement confirms the deceptiveness of the Witches' advice to Macbeth. He can now submit quietly or fight on, knowing the futility of his struggle. He raises himself to fight. The future has no real meaning for him; as his life stands, what lies ahead is a mere continuation of the present struggle.

3 **them lie** the besieging army stay

4 **ague** fever

5 **farced** reinforced

6 **dareful** boldly

10 **cooled** frozen (with fear)

11 **night-shriek** owl

fell of hair scalp

12 **dismal treatise** story of horror

14 **Direness** horrors

15 **start** startle

17 **She ... hereafter** she would have died sometime anyway, or she should have chosen some time in the future

18 **time** more appropriate time

20 **petty pace** slow speed

21 **recorded time** life (individual or human)

24 **poor player** unskilled actor

25 **struts and frets** performs boastfully and anxiously

28 **Signifying** meaning, adding up to

33 **watch** guard

36 **endure** suffer

40 **cling** wither the flesh from your bones

42 **pull in resolution** check my confidence

43 **fiend** devil

47 **avouches** alleges

48 **tarrying** remaining

50 **estate o'the world** universe

51 **wrack** destruction

52 **harness** armour

SCENE 6

[*Different editors divide the remainder of the play in different ways and it was considered more suitable in this book to deal with the remaining lines together.*]

Outside the castle the battle commences and Macbeth, surrounded, kills Young Seyward. He is sought out by Macduff while the defence of the castle collapses and finally Macbeth and Macduff prepare to fight. Macbeth claims that he is invulnerable but Macduff informs him that he, MacDuff, was not 'born' to his mother in the usual way and in the fighting Macduff kills Macbeth. When Macduff brings Macbeth's head in front of the army, Malcolm, accepted as the new king, pledges that he will bring peace and order back to Scotland.

Shakespeare tries to convey on the stage the action of the battle by having characters move on and off the centre of our attention. The focus of our attention is, of course, Macbeth. He clings to the prophecy that he cannot be harmed by one born of a woman and fights accordingly with a curious nonchalance. Although his castle has fallen behind him he fights on and seems to accept the inevitability of defeat only when the circumstances of Macduff's birth show again that the Witches told only a partial truth. He fights to the death rather than accept humiliation and we are moved by the helplessness of his final struggle. The play ends with the restoration of the order Macbeth had disrupted and a reassertion of the Christian values that Macbeth had overthrown.

4 **battle** battalion
  we the royal we
6 **order** plan
10 **clamorous harbingers** noisy announcers
11 **stake** pole (to which the bear was tied)
12 **bear-like** baiting a tied bear with dogs was a popular sport
  course attack of the dogs
26 **still** for ever
27 **kerns** Irish mercenary soldiers
28 **staves** spears
30 **undeeded** unused
32 **bruited** announced
34 **gently rendered** surrendered without a struggle
39 **strike beside us** fight with us
40 **play ... fool** commit suicide (honourable death for a defeated Roman general)
41 **lives** living men
44 **charged** burdened
47 **terms ... out** words can describe you
  losest waste
48 **intrenchant** unable to be cut
49 **impress** mark
50 **crests** helmets
51 **charmèd** protected by magic
53 **angel** devil (bad angel)
55 **Untimely ripped** abnormally delivered
57 **cowed ... man** made cowardly my manly spirit
58 **juggling** cheating
59 **palter** play (like equivocate)

63 **gaze** display

65 **Painted** advertised

68 **baited** tormented (like the bear)

rabble crowd

70 **opposed** against me

71 **try the last** fight to the death

74 **would** wish

75 **go off** die

80 **prowess confirmed** his bravery confirmed (that he was a man)

81 **unshrinking station** place from which he did not retreat

85 **before** on his front

89 **knell is knolled** death is announced

91 **parted ... score** died nobly and contributed his share

94 **time** people

95 **compassed ... pearl** surrounded by your nobles

99 **expense** extent

100 **reckon ... loves** reward your individual services

106 **snares** traps

107 **Producing forth** bringing to trial

ministers agents

110–11 **needful ... us** other necessary things demand our attention

111 **by the grace of Grace** with the help of God

112 **in measure** correctly

PART THREE

CRITICAL APPROACHES

OCCASION AND SOURCES

In 1603 James VI of Scotland became James I, King of Scotland, England and Ireland. He was a vain man, undignified, scholarly after a fashion, a generous patron of the arts. 'Kings', he said, 'are not only God's lieutenants upon earth and sit upon God's throne, but even by God himself they are called gods.' It is certain that James believed himself to have special virtues and powers because he was king. From 1604 onwards he touched people against the Evil (a skin disease called scrofula) and attributed his success to prayer. The passage in *Macbeth*, IV.3.140–59 appears to be a direct description of this practice. His interest in witchcraft and heresy is also catered for in the play. His life had been threatened by a group of witches in Scotland in 1591, and in 1605 the Gunpowder Plot had sought to blow up his government. Undoubtedly part of the concern in *Macbeth* with witchcraft and equivocation (see the Porter's speech in Act II Scene 3) relates to the topicality of these issues which the audience, and particularly King James, knew about from the trials resulting from the two plots. In 1601, Essex, and in 1603, Raleigh, two most distinguished nobles, were tried for treason and sentenced to execution.

In the 1590s Shakespeare wrote nine plays dealing with England's dynastic history. These history plays cover a large span of time and examine a wide diversity of incident and experience. Although it is a serious over-simplification to see these plays as crude propaganda for the legitimacy of Elizabeth's position as Queen, it is an undeniable truth that they were written at a very special time and appealed to patriotic, Protestant Englishmen in a very special way. The wicked Richard III who seized the throne, and held it by cruelty and deception, was a cautionary example of the danger of a bad king. The young, irresponsible Henry became, on the death of his father, Henry V, and found qualities in himself which made him a popular and heroic king. Many of Shakespeare's plays examine situations of political ambitions and power. The setting may be Rome, Alexandria, Ancient Britain,

Denmark, fifteenth-century England, or eleventh-century Scotland. Never before had a dramatist journeyed so widely for his material, but the repeated investigation indicates the contemporary fascination with the subject of political order and disorder.

For *Macbeth*, Shakespeare used the same sourcebook as he had used for the English history plays, Holinshed's *Chronicles of England, Scotland and Ireland* which was reprinted in 1587. Shakespeare never followed Holinshed slavishly but created plays based on material he found in the *Chronicles*. We can learn much about Shakespeare's dramatic intentions from the difference between his *Macbeth* and that portrayed by Holinshed. The action of the play is more tightly organised than the collection of incidents that his source offers; the characters are differentiated and developed in a manner completely unlike the original; Duncan is made into a good king and Macbeth into an almost totally brutal king; Banquo, the ancestor of King James, becomes an honest man whereas in Holinshed he helps Macbeth to murder Duncan; greater prominence is given to the Witches; and the sense of time and location is altered to suggest a concentration of action.

STRUCTURE OF THE PLAY

By the 'structure' of a play we mean how the whole play is made up of its parts and how these parts relate to each other. A play is not a gallery of portraits (the characters), nor is it a series of incidents (the plot), although both of these elements are very important. Even in a play as rich in incident as *Macbeth*, we learn most about the meaning, the total impact, of a play through the dialogue.

Macbeth is the third shortest play written by Shakespeare and one of the immediately striking aspects of it is the speed at which the action occurs. Although *Macbeth* is only two thirds of the length of *King Lear* it is divided into the same number of scenes; the scenes are very brief compared with the scenes in *King Lear*, and their brevity increases a sense of frenetic movement. It was mentioned above that Shakespeare reorganises the stories concerning Macbeth and the other characters as he found them related in Holinshed. For instance, the military action in Act I is condensed in order to demonstrate Macbeth's heroism. Always, throughout the play, the focus of our attention is fixed firmly on Macbeth. For example, in Act I Scene 5 Macbeth does not appear till after line 50, but it is his letter that Lady Macbeth reads to us and it is his character that she analyses. In Act IV Scene 3, set in the English Court, where we have a long discussion between Macduff and Malcolm on the subjects of loyalty and good kings, Macbeth is never out of our minds. We know what he has done to Macduff's family, we can see that the invented portrait Malcolm offers of himself is really a description of Macbeth, we hear the contrast between the 'good king' (Edward) and the evil Macbeth. However distant from each they may be in actual geographical terms, in the play Fife, Forres, Inverness, Scone, Dunsinane, Glamis are all brought within one day's riding time of each other and yet, because of the sense we are given of the state of Scotland and the kingship of Scotland, the size of Macbeth's ambition and the participation of the whole natural world, we feel that the struggle in the play involves a whole country and beyond that the soul of mankind. No sooner do the Witches voice a prophecy than it is fulfilled; no sooner does Macbeth inform his wife of the Witches' prophecy and she considers the possibilities than the Messenger arrives with the news that the king is coming to spend the night. In the final act the stretch of time from Lady Macbeth's sleep-walking to Macbeth's death seems to last only as long as it takes us to read the pages. This compression of time heightens our excitement and sense of suspense.

Unlike many of Shakespeare's plays, *Macbeth* has no sub-plot, or secondary action. The concentration of the play is on Macbeth. How is it, then, that the play offers so much more than the analysis of one man? One reason for this lies in the way Shakespeare juxtaposes what, in cinematic terms, would be called close-up shots and longer-range shots. Shakespeare uses the lesser characters to comment on the central action, to give a wider context to Macbeth's behaviour. Each act, with the exception of Act I, ends with such a scene where we are helped to take stock of the situation. Act III Scene 6 will serve as an example. Lennox and the unnamed Lord are not in themselves important to the play but they act as a pressure gauge to measure the tyranny of Macbeth and to register the wider significance of Macbeth's evil. The scenes with Duncan and later with Malcolm are presented as examples of decent kingly order against which Macbeth is to be judged. Equally, the scenes with the

Witches show an abyss of anti-human evil on the edge of which mankind stumbles and into which Macbeth enters.

The play operates as a series of contrasts and parallels. An important element in the texture of the play is the subtle use of **dramatic irony**. Dramatic irony occurs when a line uttered by a character has a secondary meaning noticed by the audience but not by the speaker. It also occurs when a statement or action has a special significance to the audience because of what the audience knows has happened already or anticipates will happen. Some examples should help to explain how this operates. In Act I Scene 4 lines 12–15 King Duncan says:

> There's no art
> To find the mind's construction in the face.
> He was a gentleman on whom I built
> An absolute trust.
> *Enter Macbeth, Banquo, Ross, and Angus*
> O worthiest cousin!

Duncan is talking about the treacherous Cawdor; but we know from the previous scene what thoughts are in Macbeth's mind and we apply Duncan's words to Macbeth as he enters. Duncan does not realise the full truth of his own words: the 'worthiest cousin' has prepared a most trustworthy face. In Act II Scene 2 line 67 Lady Macbeth affirms 'A little water clears us of this deed'. Later, in Act V Scene 1, walking in her sleep and making the movements of washing her hands, the conscience-tormented Lady Macbeth asks, 'What, will these hands ne'er be clean?' (line 42). When we come across the later line we remember the earlier statement and we appreciate the collapse that has taken place. If we know the play already, when we come to the line in Act II our minds move ahead to Act V and we anticipate her collapse and realise how flimsy her self-control is during the murder of Duncan.

Immediately after the murder of Duncan comes the Porter scene (Act II Scene 3). There are obscurities in this scene, possibly because of topical references readily understandable to Shakespeare's own audience but not our own. However, the main points of the scene are clear enough. The Porter imagines himself as the gatekeeper of hell and we see the ironic truth of such a claim because Macbeth has indeed made his castle a hell. The central word of the Porter's rambling talk is 'equivocator'. He welcomes to hell various deceivers, people who have played with the truth to suit their own purposes, and we recognise Macbeth as the absolute equivocator of the play, particularly in this very scene where his elaborate words seem horribly deceitful. The irony of these cross-references, however, does not stop there. In Act V, when the prophecies of the Witches which promised such safety have been exposed, Macbeth concedes that he has been the victim of equivocation as well as its instrument. In Scene 5 lines 42–4 his confidence slips:

> I pull in resolution, and begin
> To doubt the equivocation of the fiend
> That lies like truth.

Later in Scene 6 line 58, the Witches have become 'these juggling fiends'. The Porter acts as an oblique commentator on the murder and Macbeth's descent into hell. The very roughness and comedy of his act increase the gruesomeness of the murder.

IMAGERY

In a good play the dramatist seeks to make the ideas, characters and developments vivid and memorable. One way of achieving this aim is to associate, for example, a character with certain things, qualities or activities so that, when these occur, the audience remembers the character and comes to a fuller understanding of him. In Shakespeare's later plays, particularly, the **imagery** (that is, the groups of associative images) is a very important element, giving the texture of the plays density and richness. Some images, of course, are striking individually, but it is more rewarding to see the imagery as functioning in strands which help to connect, reinforce and enliven the shifts in the play as a whole. The richness of Shakespeare's imagery must inevitably suffer in translation and some is certainly lost in modern English.

The idea of contrasts lies at the heart of *Macbeth* and we intend to concentrate only on some of the strands of imagery that substantiate this interpretation. Other strands which can be followed fruitfully are those concerned with the themes of deceit, unnaturalness, killings, innocence and obligation.

ORDER AND HEALTH OPPOSED BY DISORDER AND SICKNESS

In Act I Scene 4 we have a scene of royal order when King Duncan, pleased with his success in the battle, distributes justice and rewards. Great emphasis is placed on the ties that bind a subject to his king and mutual trust is ceremoniously communicated. At the end of the scene, Duncan says (of Macbeth):

> And in his commendations I am fed;
> It is a banquet to me. Let's after him
> Whose care is gone before to bid us welcome.
> It is a peerless kinsman. (lines 56–9)

Gradually through the play we come to recognise 'banquets' as an image of order. After the supper in Macbeth's castle Duncan is described by Banquo as having been 'in unusual pleasure' (line 13) and he is now 'in measureless content'. In Act III Scene 1 Macbeth issues a special invitation to Banquo to 'a solemn supper' and when the supper begins in Scene 4 the new king is careful about the formal arrangements and the guests sit according to their 'degrees'. An intimation of disorder comes in the form of the Murderer with blood on his face, hardly a suitable guest, and when Macbeth rebukes the absent Banquo he brings disorder to the table. The supper is broken up by Lady Macbeth's command:

> Stand not upon the order of your going;
> But go at once. (lines 118–9)

The unnamed Lord in Act III Scene 6 prays that:

> we may again
> Give to our tables meat, sleep to our nights,
> Free from our feasts and banquets bloody knives,
> Do faithful homage and receive free honours – (lines 33–6)

In Act IV Scene 3 Malcolm enumerates the kingly virtues (lines 92–4) and King Edward is obviously presented as an example of a good king whose personal qualities are matched by his ability to make his people healthy. It is from this court of good order that Malcolm sets out to bring back 'wholesome days' to Scotland and the discipline and dedication evident in his army are in contrast to the morale in Dunsinane Castle.

Throughout the play there occur images of disorder and sickness. From the 'hurly-burly' of the first scene, through the 'revolt' and 'broil' of the battle, to the sense of hallucination with the Witches, we are presented with disturbances of a calm. Drunkenness is important in the first two Acts (see I.7.35, II.1.31, II.2.1–2, and the Porter scene). In Act II Macbeth comments on his 'heat-oppressed brain' (Scene 1, line 39), and his wife accuses him of being 'brain-sickly' (Scene 2, line 46). In III.1.106 Macbeth tells the Murderers that [we] 'wear our health but sickly in his [Banquo's] life' and in the following scene his wife tries to comfort him, saying 'things without all remedy / Should be without regard'. His mind is 'full of scorpions' and he is determined to bring ruin on the universe:

> Ere we will eat our meal in fear, and sleep
> In the affliction of these terrible dreams
> That shake us nightly; (III.2.17–19)

Two scenes later his lack of inner control becomes public in his 'solemn supper' when his vision of Banquo's ghost reduces him to a nervous wreck so that he breaks the 'good meeting'. Such symptoms continue throughout the remainder of the play and are shared by Lady Macbeth whose repressed conscience gives way in her sleep-walking scene.

Macbeth's personal condition is reflected in the disorder in nature on the night of Duncan's murder (see Act II Scene 4) and subsequently in a sickness in the kingdom of Scotland described to Lady Macduff by Ross (IV.2.15–22) and to Malcolm by Macduff (IV.3.4–8). The Doctor, of whom Macbeth makes such impossible demands later, says in V.1.67–8, 'unnatural deeds / Do breed unnatural troubles' and his diagnosis describes accurately the situation where the personal disorder of the king who 'cannot buckle his distempered cause / Within the belt of rule' (V.2.15–16) is reflected in his country and in the world of nature.

[Grace is used in its Christian sense of the helping power of God.]

From the moral confusion suggested by the Witches' 'Fair is foul, and foul is fair' at the beginning, the play gradually moves to show the irreconcilable distinction between good and evil. When in I.4.42–3, Duncan pronounces that 'signs of nobleness, like stars, shall shine / On all deservers', he is immediately challenged by Macbeth's private prayer:

> Stars, hide your fires,
> Let not light see my black and deep desires.
> The eye wink at the hand; yet let that be
> Which the eye fears, when it is done, to see. (lines 51–4)

In I.5.66 Lady Macbeth promises Macbeth that there shall be no sun for Duncan in the morning as a result of 'This night's great business'. Just before Macbeth enters, his wife, in words reminiscent of his in the previous scene, prays:

> Come, thick night,
> And pall thee in the dunnest smoke of hell,
> That my keen knife see not the wound it makes,
> Nor heaven peep through the blanket of the dark
> To cry, 'Hold, hold!' (1.5.48–52)

Macbeth is well aware of the sinfulness of his plan to murder Duncan and in his **soliloquy** in Scene 7 he recognises the purity of Duncan who is 'so clear in his great office' that 'his virtues / Will plead like angels' against Macbeth's use of the 'poisoned chalice', an act of complete sacrilege.

It is easier to trace the two sets of **imagery** separately but it is of fundamental importance to appreciate that they comment on each other, they together emphasise the moral force of the play in the manner shown in the previous paragraph. In Macbeth's description of the murder, the sons of the king pray for God's blessing and in Macduff's description of the murdered Duncan he is 'the Lord's anointed temple'. Banquo, who at the beginning of Act II asked for the help of the 'merciful powers' against wicked thoughts, after the murder states 'In the great hand of God I stand' (II.3.127).

In III.6.27 we are told that Malcolm has been welcomed by 'the most pious Edward with such grace' and the Scottish noblemen pray that a 'holy angel' will help to bring a blessing on Scotland. Again, as in the case of the order–disorder imagery, Act IV Scene 3 is very important in emphasising the difference between foulness and grace; Malcolm's words, lines 19–24, the description of King Edward, noted for his sanctity, and Macduff's confession of his sinfulness in lines 220–6, all demonstrate that the forces against Macbeth trust in different powers (lines 237–8) from his dark guides.

The contrary images of darkness and evil are particularly obvious in the Witches, shrewdly observed by Banquo in Act I Scene 3 to be 'the instruments of darkness'. We quickly find Macbeth invoking the foulest spirits and darkening out his conscience with images of sorcery and evil. His words immediately before the murder indicate clearly why he cannot say 'amen' during the murder. Banquo's suspicion that Macbeth had 'played most foully' to become king revives echoes of the earlier instances of 'foul', and if he were to have overheard Macbeth's self-commitment to darkness (III.2.40–56) he would have understood just how foul Macbeth's mind has become. By Act III Scene 4, after the disruption of the supper, Macbeth is stuck between darkness and day (lines 125–6) or, as he puts it:

> I am in blood
> Stepped in so far, that, should I wade no more,
> Returning were as tedious as go o'er. (lines 135–7)

Macbeth's self-identification with evil seems complete when in Act IV Scene 3 he conjures the Witches to answer his enquiries; the 'secret, black, and midnight hags' are the instruments of evil and unnaturalness, as their brew has told us, and they are addressed familiarly by something they recognise as wicked (line 45). In Act V Scene 1 Lady Macbeth concedes in her dreams that 'Hell is murky'; she who had invoked 'thick night' now requires 'light by her continually'. The Doctor declares the case needs divine care but Macbeth, obviously in a similar condition, is beyond repentance, and claims that he is beyond fear.

In the final scene of the play we find Macbeth described as a 'devil' (line 18), 'hellhound' (line 42), a follower of Satan (line 53) and a 'rarer monster' (line 64). Macbeth has killed Young Seyward, a soldier of God, according to his father who sees the war against Macbeth as a holy war against evil.

The two strands of imagery of order and grace are completed in the final
lines of the play which mark the defeat of disorder and evil:

> and what needful else
> That calls upon us, by the grace of Grace
> We will perform in measure, time, and place.
> So thanks to all at once, and to each one,
> Whom we invite to see us crowned at Scone. (V.6.110–14)

VERSE AND STYLE

Macbeth is, for the most part, written in **blank verse**. The basic unit of
blank verse is a line in **iambic** pentameter without a rhyme scheme but,
increasingly in his plays, Shakespeare's use of the line and the number of
its syllables and stresses became freer. A strict iambic pentameter has ten
syllables with the stress falling on the even ones, for example, 'And wákes
it nów to loók so gréen and pále'. Shakespeare's verse is seldom as regular
as this but the pattern is there below the changing surface resulting in
regularity with flexibility. The sense and the punctuation do not stop
dead at the end of lines but often cross into the following line, giving a
feeling of the unevenness of spoken English. By grouping stressed
syllables Shakespeare catches the emphasis and intensity of a character,
for example:

> Whiles night's black agents to their preys do rouse. (III.2.52)

where Macbeth's grim fascination with nastiness is brought out by the
voice stress on 'night's black agents'. Occasionally, Shakespeare uses
rhyming couplets. A considerable number of scenes intimate their
conclusion by this means but there are two other significant uses of
rhyme. The Witches commonly speak in rhyme, often using a shorter
line and a different stress pattern to give a sound of incantations and
charms. More interesting is the fact that Macbeth uses rhyming couplets
more often than any other character and more than the heroes of
Shakespeare's other tragedies. It does seem that he has an affinity with
the Witches.

Prose in Shakespeare's plays often denotes the low social rank of a
character, or it occurs in a situation which is abnormal, in some way, to

the ordinary behaviour of the play. In *Macbeth* there are four situations where prose is used: Macbeth's letter to his wife, Act I Scene 5; the Porter scene, Act II Scene 3; the conversation between Lady Macduff and her son, Act IV Scene 2; and the sleep-walking scene, Act V Scene 1. The reason the letter is in prose requires no explanation. What have the other three scenes in common? They all present characters who seem artless or in a state of mind where verse would appear contrived. The Porter can ramble on in his rude, somewhat incoherent way because of the amount of alcohol still in him; the mother and her child, talking of birds and traitors and fathers, soften from the formality of verse to the affectionate slackness of prose, but revert to verse when strangers enter; in her sleep-walking, Lady Macbeth loses the customary controls of verse and talks 'straight' for the first time in the play. Lady Macbeth's attendants, lower in the social scale, can talk in verse only when she has departed.

Shakespeare's characters do not voice his opinions, they speak out of their dramatic situation. That is, to understand fully a speech or an exchange of dialogue it is necessary to hear the words in their context in the play. It is impossible to deduce what Shakespeare's attitude to life was from reading Macbeth's speech in Act V Scene 5 beginning 'Tomorrow, and tomorrow, and tomorrow'. Two examples from lesser characters in different parts of the play are offered to demonstrate how necessary it is to read these pieces with proper attention to their style and context.

The first example is from Act I Scene 2 where Duncan is receiving reports from the battle fronts. The Captain is introduced to us as a 'bloody man' straight from the fight and he spends over forty lines describing the struggle of Macbeth against heavy odds. His style of reporting is breathless, lavish but crudely put together. He is weak from loss of blood and fatigue and his **syntax** is inelegant and transitions from one point to the next are sudden. But his manner is arresting – 'Mark, King of Scotland, mark!' – and at least three dramatic functions arc served well by his speech. One, the play moves off (from the short scene with the Witches) to a very exciting start; two, he comes across as the epitome of the honest, somewhat brutal soldier; three, and most important in the long term, he introduces us to Macbeth, a hero of battle, brave but a slaughterer. Contrast the manner of speech of Ross seven lines later, smoothly put together, restrained, telling what he had done for the cause of the king.

The second example is the speech of Lennox in III.6.1–20. The studied quality of the syntax tells much about the mentality of the speaker and much about the general climate of secrecy and spying in Macbeth's country. Notice the rhetorical questions to which he provides a knowing answer. We can hear the dry, ironic tone of voice of the character as he speaks. Nothing is stated directly but the speech is full of words of apparent opinion: 'gracious', 'valiant', 'monstrous', 'damned', 'pious', 'nobly', 'wisely', and so on. Macbeth's methods of deceit and sly viciousness have entered into the manner of speech of those around him. It is significant that Lennox is still serving Macbeth in Act IV Scene 1, where he says 'What's your grace's will?' and 'No, my lord' and 'Ay, my good lord'.

CHARACTERS

'Character' in a play, particularly in a Shakespearean play, is a difficult term to define. All the people, the parts, in a play form a 'list of characters' or 'dramatis personae'. Not all parts, however, are equal; some are longer than others but, although longer, they are not necessarily more important to the essential action and core of the play. Julius Caesar, for example, is not a large part in the play of that name but he influences the action throughout the play. Banquo has only a third of the lines of Malcolm but we could argue that he is a more important character because we are more aware of him, his being impinges on the action throughout the play. By character here we mean a person's essential qualities as these are manifest in the dialogue and action, and as they operate in helping to create the total effect of the play.

Shakespeare's plays are not like modern novels where the author spends a great deal of time helping us to understand how a character has come to be what he is. Often we have to accept what we are given in a Shakespearean play without asking too many questions about how the situation has been reached. The use, however, of **asides** and **soliloquies** in which a character voices his private thoughts to the audience but not to the other characters is one important way in which character is revealed. There is a psychological depth and truth in a Shakespearean play but there are also many aspects which remain untouched.

MACBETH

In the reports of Macbeth's courage in battle in the second scene of the
play, he is 'brave Macbeth' and 'valour's minion'. Duncan, acknowledging
his champion, calls him 'valiant cousin' and 'noble Macbeth'. In Act I
there is only one reservation expressed about Macbeth's character and in
different circumstances it could be considered a compliment. This
'peerless kinsman' to King Duncan is judged by his wife to have a nature
'too full o'the milk of human-kindness' (I.5.15) to allow him to kill
Duncan. She recognises his ambition to be 'great' but feels that he would
prefer to be given the throne by someone else, whatever methods were
used, rather than grab it himself. The second part of her analysis points
to a basic dishonesty in Macbeth and it is this aspect of his character that
she ruthlessly attacks to overcome his doubts in Scene 7. His qualms and
repulsion, before and after Duncan's murder, are denounced as cowardice
and foolishness by his wife and later, in Act III, she feels he has not
improved.

At the end of Act II, Macduff appears to anticipate Banquo's
suspicions that Macbeth has 'playedst most foully' to gain the throne. By
the end of Act III the decline in Macbeth's reputation is obvious; his title
of the second half of the play, 'tyrant', has been introduced. From now on
there is not a good word uttered about Macbeth. Macduff claims that:

> Not in the legions
> Of horrid hell can come a devil more damned
> In evils to top Macbeth. (IV.3.55–7)

and Malcolm asserts:

> I grant him bloody,
> Luxurious, avaricious, false, deceitful,
> Sudden, malicious, smacking of every sin
> That has a name. (IV.3.57–60)

At the end the 'cursed head' of the 'dead butcher' is displayed.

Macbeth is a soldier in armour at his first appearance in the play
and at his final exit. In between, we witness some very unsoldierly
behaviour when he is frequently out of rational control, 'rapt' and 'brain
sickly' earlier on, 'sick at heart' and 'cowed' towards the end. In situation
after situation he is preoccupied with speculations and his awareness of
this tendency leads to such resolutions as:

> Strange things I have in head, that will to hand;
> Which must be acted ere they may be scanned. (III.4.138–9)

This comes at the end of the supper scene where he has undergone excruciating tortures in his mind at the appearance of Banquo's ghost. He can act only when he does not allow himself to think and, as a result, his actions become more frenzied as the play continues. Only in Duncan's murder does he participate directly and then only under the inflexible pressure of his wife. After Duncan's and Banquo's murders come the scenes where his horror and conscience force themselves into his conscious mind to the neglect of all else. In the case of the murder of Macduff's family we do not see Macbeth again for over four hundred lines after he says, 'To crown my thoughts with acts, be it thought and done' and the terrifying callousness of the crime seems beyond his own comprehension. Each murder he commits or commissions is expected by him to end the 'restless ecstacy' he suffers but even before Duncan's murder he sees something of the futility of such an effort when he realises:

> that we but teach
> Bloody instructions, which, being taught, return
> To plague the inventor. (I.7.8–10)

Caught in a labyrinth of his own making, there is a pathetic desperation in his blustering commands:

> There is nor flying hence nor tarrying here.
> I 'gin to be aweary of the sun,
> And wish the estate o'the world were now undone. –
> Ring the alarum bell! – Blow wind, come wrack,
> At least we'll die with harness on our back. (V.5.48–52)

Macbeth lays bare his thoughts in **asides** through the play and his confusion is apparent from very early on:

> This supernatural soliciting
> Cannot be ill, cannot be good. (I.3.129–130)

and

> That function is smothered in surmise,
> And nothing is but what is not. (I.3.140–1)

We are presented with a man motivated to kill Duncan only because of ambition but who, having yielded to this desire, steps so far into blood that there is no turning back. As the play progresses we are made aware of his peculiar isolation as all escape routes are blocked off. Before Banquo's murder he tells only a certain amount of his plans to his wife who had been his 'dearest partner of greatness' and without her his reliance on the Witches becomes greater. He recognises in Act V Scene 3 that:

> that which should accompany old age,
> As honour, love, obedience, troops of friends,
> I must not look to have; (V.3.24–6)

For him, 'supped full with horrors', his wife dead, his support deserting him, life has lost all rational meaning:

> It is a tale
> Told by an idiot, full of sound and fury,
> Signifying nothing. (V.5.26–8)

We noted earlier Macbeth's association with darkness and evil, we have heard the opinions of those around him, we have witnessed his actions, and in all he is a villain. How is it, then, that we retain an interest in, possibly even a sympathy for, Macbeth? The answer must lie in the weight of evidence about him presented from the inside. We hear from his own heart of his ambition, his weakness, the wrongness of his behaviour, his deceits, and we are made aware of the intoxication he feels at his own evil. Macbeth, as a man, is weak and he finds a spurious strength in his viciousness. In his dialogue we notice a shift from a diplomatic, hollow ornateness to a blustering, bullying language full of exclamations, questions, commands, but equally hollow. In the final act Macbeth concedes to himself that his strutting and fretting are empty gestures but, chained as he is like a bear, he will not surrender and we cannot but admire his affirmation that he 'will try the last'.

LADY MACBETH

No background is offered to explain Macbeth's ambition to be king and there is a similar abruptness in the nature of Lady Macbeth as she appears in Act I Scene 5. When she reads of the Witches' prophecy in Macbeth's letter there is no indication of doubt, suspicion or hesitation in her reaction. Her one worry concerns Macbeth's ability to fulfil or enact the prophecy and she is confident that the 'valour of my tongue' will persuade him. By the time Macbeth arrives several minutes later she has mobilised her whole being towards the task of Duncan's murder. She is prepared to sacrifice her femininity and her humanity to 'give solely sovereign sway and masterdom' to Macbeth and herself.

In all the public scenes in the play she acts 'like the innocent flower'; in the private scenes we see the 'serpent under't'. She has absoluteness of purpose and discipline – her control of the situation is immaculate and we, like Macbeth, are morally paralysed by her power of will. In Act I Scene 7 we see Macbeth's feeble questions and attempts to draw back smashed aside by counter questions and a mixture of violence and practicality, which forces Macbeth into sharing her resolution and chiming in with her attitudes and words. In the scene of the murder there is a sharp contrast between the rambling, whining narration of Macbeth and the snapping, categorical rebukes and practical detail of his wife. Macbeth is stuck in his own imagination; she refuses to see anything but the immediate actions.

She manages to maintain this control over herself during the supper scene with Banquo's ghost, but earlier, in Act III Scene 2 we have heard her first private thought since the murder of Duncan:

> Naught's had, all's spent,
> Where our desire is got without content.
> 'Tis safer to be that which we destroy
> Than by destruction dwell in doubtful joy. (lines 4–7)

Macbeth enters at this point and she changes her attitude immediately, attempting to eradicate in Macbeth what we know she feels in herself. It is noticeable in this scene that after her initial words of comfort, she is allowed no time to speak by Macbeth and for the first time we hear her say 'What's to be done?'. She does not know of Macbeth's plans for Banquo, and planning has passed from her hands to Macbeth.

After the supper scene – where, incidentally, we notice after the departure of the guests Macbeth again shows his leadership – Lady Macbeth appears only once, in her sleep-walking scene at the beginning of Act V. This scene is very important to the play structurally because it summarises the murders of Macbeth before Malcolm's assault and the confession comes from his 'fiend-like queen' herself. But the questions that intrigue readers are: Why has Lady Macbeth collapsed from her position in Act I? What has happened to the rigid self-discipline? The answer seems to lie in the very rigidity of her self-discipline. Macbeth, who started from a weaker position, has had some release in his own imaginings; he has confessed to the ugliness of his deeds and has gradually come to accept his precarious stance. His wife has only once in our hearing suggested that her contentment is incomplete. Gradually, in her case, her repressed conscience and her knowledge that the 'sovereign sway and masterdom' have not materialised have forced themselves into her dreams so that now, as the doctor says, she re-enacts the murders in her mind in sleep. The contrast between her curt assurance in Act II Scene 2 and her foulness in Act V Scene 1 is painfully ironic. Her suicide is the final desperate act of the mind seeking to cleanse itself:

> 'Tis safer to be that which we destroy
> Than by destruction dwell in doubtful joy. (III.2.6–7)

BANQUO

For the first half of the play, Banquo is very obviously presented by Shakespeare as a parallel figure to Macbeth. Both distinguish themselves by fighting for their king, both have promises made to them by the Witches, but there the similarity ends. Banquo's reply to the king's praise is brief and self-effacing; Macbeth's is fuller and, from our knowledge of Macbeth's thoughts in the previous scene, we suspect it is dishonest.

In the previous scene, Act I Scene 3, Banquo's reaction to the Witches is noticeably more casual than Macbeth's, but Banquo does ask the Witches if they see anything in the future for him. In their equivocal replies they promise him greatness and happiness, in comparison with Macbeth. In the play he is morally superior to Macbeth and he is not unhappy in the tortured manner of Macbeth. The Witches' significant prediction, however, is that his descendants will become kings. Both men are genuinely startled at the immediate fulfilment of the prediction that Macbeth will become Thane of Cawdor, but Banquo's puzzlement takes

the form of scepticism and a deep distrust of the Witches whom he sees
as the 'devil' or the 'instruments of darkness'. This distrust later becomes
fear when, in Act II Scene 1, he tells of the 'cursed thoughts that nature
gives way to in repose' and we find out in line 20 that he has been
dreaming of the Witches. Unlike Macbeth, he prays for God's help
('merciful powers') against whatever 'cursed thoughts' he has; in Christian
doctrine sin takes place when temptation is yielded to, not when
temptation occurs. We have seen Macbeth examining his temptation in
his **soliloquy** at the beginning of the previous scene, but by the time
Banquo is in bed, it is obvious to the audience that Macbeth is entering
knowingly into a world of darkness and sorcery.

Macbeth is taunted by two aspects of Banquo which he explains in
III.1.48–71. The virtue, the strength of character, of Banquo is a rebuke
to Macbeth's weaker character and Macbeth cannot tolerate the thought
that he has sacrificed his soul to profit Banquo by allowing the latter's
descendants to become kings. These two aspects remain to torment
Macbeth's mind after the murder of Banquo and the escape of Fleance.
Banquo's ghost arrives when summoned by Macbeth's conscience: when
Macbeth tries to dismiss Banquo with words, the ghost comes to rebuke
him. Macbeth's impotent rage at the survival of Banquo's line in the
Witches' Show of eight kings expresses itself in the massacre of Macduff's
'wife, his babes, and all unfortunate souls / That trace him in his line'.

THE WITCHES

The Witches are the instruments of malevolent forces which seek to lead
men away from goodness. Macbeth is peculiarly vulnerable to their
influence because he hears them voice the desires of his mind and after
his initial fear at being caught out (I.3.50–1) his mind moves easily along
the route they indicate towards the 'imperial theme'. The Witches' nature
is continually evoked and invoked in speeches by Macbeth and Lady
Macbeth and their very sexlessness (I.3.44–6) seems to correspond with
Lady Macbeth's prayer against her own nature in I.5.38–52.

Macbeth is able to find them when he chooses later on but he wants
to hear only what favours himself. Too late he comes to realise that the
Witches have their own purposes into which men fit and which men can
serve. The equivocation theme which is central to the play operates most

obviously through the Witches and they are the most striking voices of unnaturalness and disorder. Lady Macbeth offers no comment on the Witches, the 'metaphysical aid', who promise so much to her husband. It is Macbeth who needs the Witches to tell him what is in his own mind but what he is afraid to acknowledge as his own. The Witches, of course, do not make promises; they utter riddles which Macbeth in his weakness interprets in his own apparent interest. He is, therefore, not deceived by the Witches but by his ill-founded reliance on his own interpretation:

> He shall spurn fate, scorn death, and bear
> His hopes 'bove wisdom, grace, and fear.
> And you all know security
> Is mortals' chiefest enemy. (III.5.30–3)

MACDUFF

With his knocking at the gate, Macduff is the first intrusion of the outside world on Macbeth's murder of Duncan. Through the remainder of the play he continues to annoy and challenge Macbeth and in II.4.37–8 we hear the first suspicion of Macbeth when Macduff, having decided not to attend Macbeth's coronation, suggests that the new regime may not be a comfortable one. He keeps clear of Macbeth's 'solemn supper' and at the end of the supper scene Macbeth's plans of further murders seem to include the uncooperative Macduff, plans which receive confirmation from his visit to the Witches. Shakespeare's handling of the scene in Macduff's castle emphasises the family affection and the vulnerability of Lady Macduff and her son left defenceless by the absence of Macduff. Macduff's act of political bravery, in effect, sacrifices his innocent family to the brutality of tyranny. His bravery and honesty emerge in the long scene with Malcolm and in the end it is a poetic justice that Macduff should be the one to execute Macbeth. The final confrontation brings from Macbeth his only public confession of guilt when he says in V.6.44–5 'my soul is too much charged / With blood of thine already'.

DUNCAN

Duncan is murdered in Act II Scene 2, but in the eight scenes before that he has met Macbeth only once. Macbeth himself seems to avoid the king as much as possible so that it is Lady Macbeth who welcomes Duncan to Inverness and Macbeth does not even remain in the supper room with the king. Duncan is presented to us as a dignified, gentle and appreciative ruler. Macbeth is aware of Duncan's virtues and sees the enormity of his proposed murder of him. Act I Scene 6 offers a picture of peace and trust in complete contrast to Scene 5 and the second half of Scene 7, and even Lady Macbeth sees a likeness to her own father in Duncan's sleeping face. Macbeth does not, cannot, describe the act of murdering Duncan; his hand seems to do a deed independently of his troubled mind. The treachery and deceit of Macbeth and Lady Macbeth are apparent in the ways they avoid calling the murder by its name but speak of 'business', 'provided for', 'deed', 'it', 'quell'. Macbeth's theatrical description of Duncan in II.3.108–13 seems in its very ornateness to evade the horror. The nastiness of the murder is most fully felt in Lady Macbeth's chilling question much later: 'Yet who would have thought the old man to have had so much blood in him?' (V.1.38–9).

MALCOLM

The flight of Malcolm after the murder of his father seems very sudden from the evidence given in the play. He is the chosen heir but he seems immediately to suspect that the fate of his father may come to him as well. In the early part of the play he is a dutiful attendant to his father. In his meeting with Macduff in Act IV Scene 3, he reveals himself as a shrewd politician unwilling to commit himself till the evidence is clear. He tests Macduff's honesty, at the same time as presenting himself as the very opposite of Macbeth. In the final act he is the instrument by which good government is to be restored to Scotland (with the help of England) and his deference to law and order is apparent not only in his final speech but, in the scenes leading up to the battle, in his willingness to bow to the knowledge of more experienced men. The connection between his style of speaking in his final speech and his father's manner in Act I Scene 4 demonstrates the reassertion of virtue in the person of the king.

Macbeth is a play about the fall of a good man and his belated realisation of his corruption. In Shakespeare's scheme of events the wellbeing of a country is at the mercy of the wellbeing of the ruler. The Porter and the Old Man and Ross may reflect on the disorder around them but they seem helpless to check such an upheaval:

> Alas, poor country,
> Almost afraid to know itself! It cannot
> Be called our mother, but our grave; where nothing
> But who knows nothing is once seen to smile;
> Where sighs and groans and shrieks that rent the air
> Are made, not marked; where violent sorrow seems
> A modern ecstasy. (IV.3.164–70)

A new morality personified in Malcolm is needed to supplant evil. Macbeth's tyranny is the practice of devilish wickedness, his advisers are the 'instruments of darkness' and his unnatural rule can be opposed only with the help of the Christian God.

That, it seems, is the metaphysical framework erected by the structure and **imagery** of the play, but the meaning of the work is *not* limited to such a theological interpretation. The play is, in many respects, like its **Morality** predecessors, but Shakespeare's construction of his hero gives a new dimension to the struggle between good and evil. Macbeth is a nobleman, a good soldier, but these qualities are a mere surface in comparison with what we learn of his mind. He impresses us as an individual with his own complex and idiosyncratic way of seeing the world. We do not comprehend the reasons for his ambition but through his (and Shakespeare's) poetry we enter his hell with him. In the play the concept of man occurs in a number of places and for us the concept is humanised, individualised by Macbeth's experience. In Act I, Macbeth is fully aware of the danger his 'single state of man' is in and with the softness of his 'human kindness' he pronounces:

> I dare do all that may become a man;
> Who dares do more is none. (1.7.46–7)

By the end of the Act, however, he is taunted with his unmanliness by his wife, who is herself prepared to be dehumanised. He is taunted to such an extent that he is prepared to 'bend up / Each corporal agent to this terrible deed', but when the deed is done he says 'To know my deed 'twere best not know myself'. The battle for his self-esteem is won and lost. He now comes to fear Banquo's 'being' (III.1.54) because of the latter's 'royalty of nature', and in his encounter with Banquo's ghost he becomes 'unmanned in folly', according to his wife. His courage can cope only with the physical; for any human attribute beyond the physical he feels fear or cynicism. The life of man is reduced to a procession of 'fools', a 'walking shadow', a performance of make-believe, the mouthing of an idiot. The humanity of Macduff's reaction to the news of his family's killing – 'but I must also feel it as a man' – is a contrast that controls the conclusion of the play. We see the torment and the emptiness of Macbeth's life and we turn with relief to the dignity and humanity of Macduff and the order re-established by Malcolm. Macbeth, the usurper, the overreacher against these values, is exposed as a dwarfish thief in a giant's robe (see V.2.20–2).

Macbeth's murder of King Duncan is not simply an act of political rebellion but, as he recognises in his **soliloquy**, I.7.1–28, a violation of all the laws of hospitality, kinship and human decency. To Shakespeare's contemporaries the play must have offered a penetrating analysis of personal aspiration and political ambition. Even a good man, and the early reports in the play suggest that Macbeth had fine qualities, is pathetically vulnerable to the seductive and destructive possibilities of power.

Part four

Textual analysis

TEXT 1 (II.1.31–64)

MACBETH:

Go bid thy mistress, when my drink is ready
She strike upon the bell. Get thee to bed.

Exit servant

Is this a dagger which I see before me,
The handle toward my hand? Come, let me clutch thee –
I have thee not and yet I see thee still!
Art thou not, fatal vision, sensible
To feeling as to sight? Or art thou but
A dagger of the mind, a false creation,
Proceeding from the heat-oppressèd brain?
I see thee yet, in form as palpable   40
As this which now I draw.
Thou marshall'st me the way that I was going,
And such an instrument I was to use. –
Mine eyes are made the fools o'the other senses,
Or else worth all the rest. – I see thee still;
And, on thy blade and dudgeon, gouts of blood,
Which was not so before. There's no such thing.
It is the bloody business which informs
Thus to mine eyes. Now o'er the one half-world
Nature seems dead, and wicked dreams abuse   50
The curtained sleep. Witchcraft celebrates
Pale Hecat's offerings; and withered Murder,
Alarumed by his sentinel the wolf,
Whose howl's his watch, thus with his stealthy pace,
With Tarquin's ravishing strides, towards his design
Moves like a ghost. Thou sure and firm-set earth,
Hear not my steps, which way they walk, for fear
Thy very stones prate of my whereabout
And take the present horror from the time

Which now suits with it. – Whiles I threat, he lives: 60
Words to the heat of deeds too cold breath gives.
   A bell rings
I go, and it is done; the bell invites me.
Hear it not, Duncan, for it is a knell
That summons thee to heaven or to hell.   *Exit*

FORM OF THE PASSAGE

The passage is in verse, apparently regular. There is only one interruption (the bell) and there is only one character present, Macbeth. The fact that the passage is a **soliloquy** is important because it means that what we are hearing is heard by no other character in the play and Macbeth can speak his mind frankly – he has nobody to deceive but himself.

CONTEXT OF THE PASSAGE

Despite the customary act division, there is no obvious break in time between the beginning of Act I Scene 7 and the end of Act II Scene 3. The soliloquy comes after the supper guests have retired to bed and immediately before the murder of Duncan. In Act I Scene 7 we heard Macbeth wrestling with his conscience and finally being forced into preparedness by the forcefulness of his wife. Immediately after the murder Macbeth is almost helpless with anxiety and cannot pull his mind away from his experience in Duncan's bedroom. By Act II Scene 3 he has partially recovered although his speech in lines 88–93 seems to hark back to Act I Scene 7.

This placing of the soliloquy may seem over-elaborate but no scene in a play operates independently of others around it, and our awareness of this context gives added richness to the particular passage. Two examples are sufficient for the moment. At the end of Act I Scene 7 Macbeth says, imitating the resolution and earlier words of his wife:

I am settled; and bend up
Each corporal agent to this terrible feat.
Away, and mock the time with fairest show:
False face must hide what the false heart doth know. (lines 79–82)

Some time later, he declines to discuss the Witches with Banquo. Now in the soliloquy, we hear the thoughts of this 'settled' man who claims that he does not think of the Witches. His soliloquy is revealing in showing that Macbeth's control is not very firm. Left on his own, his mind imagines things and he cannot hold his imagination in check. The other example of the significance of the context looks forward to the following scene where his self-control has collapsed, and the incident of murdering Duncan is filled with noises so that he pleads, 'How is't with me when every noise appals me?'. Now look again at the lines 56–60 of the soliloquy and beyond those to lines 16–25 of Act I Scene 7.

CHARACTER REVEALED IN THE PASSAGE

The soliloquy is Macbeth's final preparation of himself before the murder. What might we expect him to think about? The plan? The fear of discovery? What he must do as soon as the murder is committed? None of these things is spoken of directly by Macbeth; in fact, his thoughts seem to operate at a tangent to the deed ahead.

He does not wonder about the difficulty of the task but he uses his imagination to shift his mind from the actual. Where does his imagined dagger come from? It seems to have a will of its own, 'Thou marshall'st me'. Macbeth pushes the dagger from his mind and replaces it with an atmosphere suitable to his intention and appropriate company (the figures of Murder, the wolf and Tarquin). Only when his mind is so prepared is he ready to act, to act as an automaton. He has become an instrument hypnotised by himself to act when he receives the signal.

STYLE OF THE PASSAGE

(a) ORGANISATION
There are four units in the **soliloquy**: lines 33–49 concerning the dagger; lines 49–56, voicing Macbeth's reverie on the world outside; lines 56–60, an invocation to the earth; lines 60–4, he moves into action. How does Macbeth's mind move from one unit to the next? The dagger arrives suddenly in the air and in line 48 Macbeth exerts his reason and attributes the appearance of the dagger to his preoccupation with the murder plan. The second unit is the result of Macbeth looking away from the dagger but his thoughts remain obstinately on the idea of the murder. The word 'Nature' should be a contrary force to his hallucination but it 'seems dead'

and allows 'wicked dreams' to deceive sleeping man. Macbeth is still hallucinating. The ghost-like movement of Murder stalking his victim leads into the insistence on quietness in the third unit. The final unit is a break from the preceding lines. Here Macbeth repeats instructions to himself as if still unsure of what he is doing. Notice also that the threats he refers to have not taken place very solidly but he has filled in the time while awaiting the signal without losing his nerve. It is significant that Macbeth does not mention any person around him, not even his wife, and that he avoids naming his victim till the second last line.

(b) IMAGERY
This is not a heavily **metaphorical** piece like some that occur elsewhere in the play but there are some interesting choices of language. There is a move from sights to sounds in the soliloquy matching the furtiveness and tension of Macbeth. Human beings (but Macbeth really means himself) are strangely passive: the dagger offers its handle; it indicates directions; the eyes are made fools of; the 'bloody business' 'informs' and dreams 'abuse'; the bell 'invites' or 'summons'. Of course, the dagger itself with its suggestive movements and drops of blood is an image of Macbeth's troubled conscience which he cannot control ('clutch') or be sure about. The 'heat-oppressèd brain' which creates the elusive dagger is the same brain that is needed for the 'heat of deeds'. In the **imagery** of witchcraft and murder the concentration is on the sacrifice of innocence (the 'curtained sleep' and the pure Lucretia) by a secret and ruthless power. The only colours present in the soliloquy are those of darkness and blood.

(c) SYNTAX AND PUNCTUATION
What is immediately noticeable is that the first and fourth units have different lengths of sentences from the middle units. Added together the first and fourth have about twelve sentences; the second and third have two or three. The first unit is marked by questions, exclamations, qualifications, repetitions, all suggesting uncertainty and jumpiness. The lines and sentences are sub-divided so that, in reading them, one has a sense of Macbeth's unease. The final unit gives an impression of resolution but the resolution is so repeated and so tidily arranged that we suspect something glib and mechanical in it. In the middle units with their longer sentences we receive a sense of deliberation and suspense, as

if we have to hold our breath to read right through the sentences. There are more adjectives than in the other units and they give intensity to the thought. In the first and fourth units, also, there is a frequent mention of 'I', 'me', 'my', but in the middle units the word 'my' occurs twice only. This fits with the general words in these middle units: 'Nature', 'dreams', 'Witchcraft', 'Murder' against whom individual man seems helpless. The whole soliloquy is in the present tense except for 'was' in lines 42, 43 and 47. Macbeth seems unable to think of either the past or the future; he is rapt in the 'present horror'.

(d) Verse

The rhythm of the soliloquy coincides very closely with the **syntax** and we have a clear sound of Macbeth's doubts in the earlier part giving way to the measured strides of Murder. Notice the stress coming on the opening syllable of line 56, 'Moves like a ghost'; after the descriptive phrases, Murder approaches its victim firmly, inevitably. The stress falls, for the most part, on the final syllable of the line, and as the quietness intensifies in the soliloquy this stress becomes more noticed until at the end, Macbeth's mechanical resolution finds help in rhyming couplets. Notice also in the final five lines the repetition of vowel sounds particularly in 'threat', 'breath', 'bell', 'knell', 'Heaven', 'Hell'; and 'he', 'heat', 'deeds', 'me', 'hear', 'thee', which give a complex crosspattern of sounds and words pulling the lines together and forcing the sense on our ears.

TEXT 2   (III.4.82–143)

LADY: My worthy lord,
Your noble friends do lack you.
MACBETH: I do forget.
Do not muse at me, my most worthy friends:
I have a strange infirmity, which is nothing
To those that know me. Come, love and health to all!
Then I'll sit down. Give me some wine; fill full!
    Enter Ghost
I drink to the general joy o'the whole table,

And to our dear friend Banquo, whom we miss.
Would he were here! To all – and him – we thirst,   90
And all to all.
Lords: Our duties and the pledge!
Macbeth: (*sees the Ghost*)
Avaunt, and quit my sight! Let the earth hide thee!
Thy bones are marrowless, thy blood is cold.
Thou hast no speculation in those eyes
Which thou dost glare with.
Lady: Think of this, good peers,
But as a thing of custom; 'tis no other;
Only it spoils the pleasure of the time.
Macbeth:
What man dare, I dare.
Approach thou like the rugged Russian bear,
The armed rhinoceros, or the Hyrcan tiger,   100
Take any shape but that, and my firm nerves
Shall never tremble. Or be alive again,
And dare me to the desert with thy sword:
If trembling I inhabit then, protest me
The baby of a girl. Hence, horrible shadow!
Unreal mockery, hence!   *Exit Ghost*
                          Why, so; being gone,
I am a man again. – Pray you sit still.
lady:
You have displaced the mirth, broke the good meeting
With most admired disorder.
Macbeth: Can such things be,
And overcome us like a summer's cloud,   110
Without our special wonder? You make me strange
Even to the disposition that I owe
When now I think you can behold such sights
And keep the natural ruby of your cheeks,
When mine is blanched with fear.
Ross: What sights, my lord?
Lady:
I pray you speak not; he grows worse and worse.

Question enrages him. At once, good night.
Stand not upon the order of your going;
But go at once.
LENNOX: Good night; and better health
Attend his majesty!
LADY: A kind good-night to all!   *Exeunt Lords*   120
MACBETH:
It will have blood, they say; blood will have blood.
Stones have been known to move and trees to speak;
Augurs and understood relations have
By maggot-pies, and choughs, and rooks brought forth
The secret'st man of blood. What is the night?
LADY:
Almost at odds with morning, which is which.
MACBETH:
How sayst thou, that Macduff denies his person
At our great bidding?
LADY: Did you send to him, sir?
MACBETH:
I hear it by the way. But I will send.
There's not a one of them, but in his house   130
I keep a servant fee'd. I will tomorrow –
And betimes I will – to the Weird Sisters.
More shall they speak; for now I am bent to know
By the worst means the worst. For mine own good
All causes shall give way. I am in blood
Stepped in so far, that, should I wade no more,
Returning were as tedious as go o'er.
Strange things I have in head, that will to hand;
Which must be acted ere they may be scanned.
LADY:
You lack the season of all natures, sleep.   140
MACBETH:
Come, we'll to sleep. My strange and self-abuse
Is the initiate fear that wants hard use.
We are yet but young in deed.   *Exeunt*

FORM OF THE PASSAGE

The passage comes from a scene which is, for most of the time, crowded with people. In the final twenty lines, Macbeth and Lady Macbeth are on their own. In the whole passage, four characters speak and there is a line of response from the assembled crowd. However, there is also the ghost of Banquo, visible only to Macbeth. The dialogue between characters and the speeches remain in **blank verse** till line 134 when rhyme takes over.

CONTEXT OF THE PASSAGE

Act III Scene 4 is in the very middle of the play but there are some unusual features for a scene in such a position. The opening of the scene sees Macbeth at the height of his new power; his situation deteriorates from this point. Lady Macbeth, who seems such a central character in the drama, is to appear only once more in the play (V.I), briefly and in her sleep. The proportions of the play may appear odd, as if the climax has come too early. We need to think why Shakespeare has constructed his play in this way.

Between Acts II and III there is a lapse of time: Macbeth has been crowned king but Banquo, for whose descendants the Witches had offered favourable predictions, still lives and, while he does, presents a threat to Macbeth's future. By the beginning of Scene 3 we know what Macbeth does not, that Banquo has been murdered but that Fleance has escaped. The opening of the scene shows Macbeth as the masterful and hospitable king: the banquet, because we have not seen his coronation at Scone, is a formal confirmation of his status. The first twelve lines emphasise welcome and order but a different note is struck in line 13: 'There's blood upon thy face!'. This disquieting note is reiterated and magnified with the appearance, to Macbeth, of Banquo's ghost. The particular passage under discussion occurs after the disappearance of the ghost, when Macbeth is striving to regain his composure; and in the passage the ghost of Banquo reappears.

Towards the end of the passage Macbeth declares his intention to seek out the Witches and, as if he has conjured them, they immediately appear in the following Scene (III.5). With a peculiar irony, Lady Macbeth's final words in the Scene: 'You lack the season of all natures, sleep', anticipate her next and final appearance in the play (V.1) when she walks and talks in her sleep. The unravelling of Macbeth's forced self-discipline in the passage intimates his eventual disintegration.

CHARACTER REVEALED IN THE PASSAGE

Although the scene involves many people, the focus is clearly on Macbeth and how he copes with the appearance of Banquo who has just been murdered on his instructions. Whatever theory we may have about ghosts, the appearance of Banquo is real to Macbeth but only he sees it. What most frightens him is the unnaturalness of the thing; it is recognisably Banquo but it is dead: 'Thy bones are marrowless, thy blood is cold. / Thou hast no speculation in those eyes' (lines 93–4). If he could fight physically with it, he would not be afraid but it is a 'horrible shadow', an 'Unreal mockery'. Macbeth's guilt and imagination combine to see the ghost as an unstoppable force of vengeance; and, even after it has disappeared, he sees it in a paranoid way as seeking him out with the help of natural agents to have his blood in return for the blood he has shed (lines 123–7). His emphasis on 'man' works in two senses: 'man' as human and 'man' as male. The second sense recalls his wife's taunts in Act I Scene 7 and it is she in the present scene who first challenges his manhood: 'Are you a man?' (line 57) and, 'What, quite unmanned in folly?' (line 72). As happened in the earlier scene she has to cajole and organise him through his difficulties, and in both scenes she appears more composed, more in control. It is she who first explains away his violent reaction to the ghost by claiming that he has, since childhood, periodically suffered from what Macbeth later describes as 'a strange infirmity' (line 85). Macbeth is thrown into complete confusion so that he no longer is sure who or what he is (lines 111–12). After Lady Macbeth has ushered out the guests, Macbeth has to reassert himself and in his speech in lines 129–39 he speaks as if to himself. The word 'I' is repeated nine times and his wife seems excluded till the 'we' in line 141. In the speech he shakes off his fears and irresolution and proclaims an extreme line of action: 'For mine own good / All causes shall give way'. In the final lines of the scene his confidence has returned and he seems to laugh off the business with the ghost as simple inexperience in crime, something he aims to sort out very soon, after seeking the advice of the Witches.

STYLE OF THE PASSAGE

(a) ORGANISATION

One way to see the arrangement of the passage is as inward and outward movements centred on Macbeth. It opens with Lady Macbeth recalling him from his musings to his duties as a host to the guests. Ten lines later, with the reappearance of the ghost, he is again absent from the banquet, shut in with his guilty imaginings. When the ghost disappears he tries to emerge (line 107) but he cannot easily shake off the questions in his mind. In line 125 he suddenly returns to actuality with 'What is the night?' His interchange with his wife is only partly a conversation until the 'we' in line 141. Although, across the whole passage, Macbeth has three times the number of lines given to his wife, they both speak eight times. The emphasis is firmly on him but she is needed to push the scene forward and to mediate between him and the guests. The introduction of the ghost several lines before it is seen by Macbeth emphasises the hypocrisy of his toast to 'our dear friend Banquo'. Later, the scrambled departure of the guests ('Stand not upon the order of your going') only a few lines after Macbeth has asked 'Pray you sit still' demonstrates the disruption of what should have been a formal coronation feast.

(b) IMAGERY

Probably the most obvious strand of **imagery** stems from the situation in the scene. A banquet is organised, has a formality in seating arrangements and ordering of courses, and gives a sense of occasion. The scene opens with full awareness of the formality: 'You know your own degrees, sit down' (line 1) and Macbeth and Lady Macbeth as 'host' and 'hostess'. The disorder that ensues and Macbeth's frantic efforts to restore conviviality: 'I drink to the general joy o'the whole table' (line 88), reveal the hollowness of Macbeth's hospitality. Macbeth is shown to be ill: 'he grows worse and worse' (line 116) and his disorder is reflected in how he sees nature: 'Stones have been known to move and trees to speak' (line 122). There is a reiteration in the vocabulary of this disorder: 'infirmity', 'spoils', 'tremble', 'unreal', 'displaced', 'broke', 'disorder', 'overcome', 'at odds', 'lack' and 'self-abuse'. The second strand of imagery relates to blood and bloodlessness. The blood which has been stabbed out of Banquo obsesses Macbeth throughout the scene. Even the ghost's hair seems 'gory' when he first appears and his second appearance comes immediately after Macbeth's call: 'Give me some wine; fill full' (line 87). The redness of blood and the paleness of the ghost indicate a contrast between life and death and, in the passage, a conflict between the two: 'blood will have blood' (line 121); it is as if Banquo's ghost has come to seek Macbeth's blood: his cheeks have lost their 'natural ruby' and are 'blanched with fear'. Macbeth, as the murderer, becomes the 'man of blood' and he sees himself wading in blood. The third strand of imagery has been discussed above and concerns manness or manliness. The arrival of the ghost unmans Macbeth but it also causes him to question his beliefs about life and death: 'The times has been / That, when the brains were out, the man would die, / And there an end. But now they rise again' (lines 77–9). The word 'strange' recurs through the passage, emphasising the disintegration of Macbeth's previously firm categories of men and ghosts, men and children (or dolls), courage and cowardice, sanity and insanity.

(c) SYNTAX AND PUNCTUATION

In the passage the speech of the attendant lords is mechanical, dutiful, predictable and minimal. Lady Macbeth's function in the passage is to rescue her husband and re-establish some normality. Her pieces of dialogue are short and to the point, a series of statements and urgent requests; the urgency is apparent in her longest speech (lines 116–19) where her three and a half lines are broken into six terse units, culminating in a desperate or rude command: 'But go at once'. Macbeth's speech is much more varied, as he struggles to regain control of himself and come to terms with what has taken place. His struggle is obvious in the opening speech of the passage where, in his rush to sound normal, he becomes almost incoherent. Lines 86–91 are made up of jerky phrases, reflecting his upset mind; in line 90 he exclaims, 'we thirst' when he means 'we drink' and he ends his toast with the circular 'And all to all'. His speech is marked with exclamations and questions, and his impassioned, fevered address to the ghost, invisible to all but himself, conveys his confusion and guilt. When Ross demands: 'What sights, my Lord?', Lady Macbeth intervenes quickly to prevent her husband from further incriminating himself. Macbeth often speaks in parallel phrases as if making stabs at understanding what he finds incomprehensible. He yanks himself back towards normality with his question: 'What is the night?' and his **syntax** calms down into dogged determination in lines 131–9.

(d) Verse

It is significant that in lines 82 and 95, Lady Macbeth speaks the second half of a line as if she is frightened to let her husband continue; she diverts the proceedings. Generally, the verse follows an **iambic** pentameter pattern and the metre has no obvious peculiarities or lapses. An oddity does take place in the final ten lines. Macbeth departs from the **blank verse** (unrhymed) to speak in rhyming couplets. As is discussed elsewhere, Macbeth sometimes does move into rhyme throughout the play. In this instance, it is worth noting that he has just mentioned the Witches and they habitually speak in rhymed couplets; a link does seem to exist between the Witches and Macbeth. The use of rhymed couplets here gives a measured tread to Macbeth's resolve. He sounds hypnotised by something in his mind, something which he only half understands:

> Strange things I have in head, that will to hand;
> Which must be acted ere they may be scanned.

The rhyme, the regularity of the metre, and the balancing of the two halves of each line, give a rhetorical assurance to his statement.

TEXT 3 (IV.3.31–100)

MACDUFF: Bleed, bleed, poor country!
Great Tyranny, lay thou thy basis sure,
For goodness dare not check thee; wear thou thy wrongs,
The title is affeered. Fare thee well, lord! .
I would not be the villain that thou think'st
For the whole space that's in the tyrant's grasp,
And the rich East to boot.
MALCOLM: Be not offended;
I speak not as in absolute fear of you.
I think our country sinks beneath the yoke,

It weeps, it bleeds, and each new day a gash   40
Is added to her wounds. I think withal
There would be hands uplifted in my right;
And here from gracious England have I offer
Of goodly thousands. But for all this,
When I shall tread upon the tyrant's head
Or wear it on my sword, yet my poor country
Shall have more vices than it had before,
More suffer, and more sundry ways, than ever,
By him that shall succeed.

MACDUFF: What should he be?

MALCOLM:

It is myself I mean; in whom I know   50
All the particulars of vice so grafted
That, when they shall be opened, black Macbeth
Will seem as pure as snow and the poor state
Esteem him as a lamb, being compared
With my confineless harms.

MACDUFF: Not in the legions
Of horrid hell can come a devil more damned
In evils to top Macbeth.

MALCOLM: I grant him bloody,
Luxurious, avaricious, false, deceitful,
Sudden, malicious, smacking of every sin
That has a name. But there's no bottom, none,   60
In my voluptuousness. Your wives, your daughters,
Your matrons, and your maids, could not fill up
The cistern of my lust; and my desire
All continent impediments would o'erbear
That did oppose my will. Better Macbeth
Than such a one to reign.

MACDUFF: Boundless intemperance
In nature is a tyranny. It hath been
The untimely emptying of the happy throne,
And fall of many kings. But fear not yet
To take upon you what is yours. You may   70
Convey your pleasures in a spacious plenty

And yet seem cold; the time you may so hoodwink.
We have willing dames enough. There cannot be
That vulture in you to devour so many
As will to greatness dedicate themselves,
Finding it so inclined.
MALCOLM: With this there grows
In my most ill-composed affection such
A staunchless avarice that, were I king,
I should cut off the nobles for their lands,
Desire his jewels and this other's house,   80
And my more-having would be as a sauce
To make me hunger more, that I should forge
Quarrels unjust against the good and loyal,
Destroying them for wealth.
MACDUFF: This avarice
Sticks deeper, grows with more pernicious root
Than summer-seeming lust; and it hath been
The sword of our slain kings. Yet do not fear:
Scotland hath foisons to fill up your will
Of your mere own. All these are portable,
With other graces weighed.
MALCOLM: But I have none.   90
The king-becoming graces,
As justice, verity, temperance, stableness,
Bounty, perseverance, mercy, lowliness,
Devotion, patience, courage, fortitude,
I have no relish of them, but abound
In the division of each several crime,
Acting it many ways. Nay, had I power, I should
Pour the sweet milk of concord into hell,
Uproar the universal peace, confound
All unity on earth.
MACDUFF: O Scotland, Scotland!   100

FORM OF THE PASSAGE

This seems a very ordinary part of the play: two men, Malcolm and Macduff, are conversing and there is no action. Nobody enters or exits. The **blank verse** is regular and there are no abrupt shifts or interruptions. No voice is raised and there are no stage-directions.

CONTEXT OF THE PASSAGE

The lines occur in the longest scene in *Macbeth*, and the first half of the scene poses problems for any production because it is so static and seems, in its length, out of proportion to the rest of a very busy play. The scene, the only one set outside Scotland, sits between two of the most theatrical scenes in the play: the murder of Macduff's family and Lady Macbeth's sleep-walking. Macbeth himself, although he is so much the centre of attention in the play, is not on stage from the end of Act IV Scene 1 till Act V Scene 3. The scene from which we have chosen our passage draws back from the action around Macbeth and offers views on his situation from a perspective outside that situation. We see Malcolm as an aspirant king against Macbeth; we see King Edward of England as a saintly and beneficent ruler, a healer in contrast to Macbeth; and we see Macduff's grief as genuine and not political. When we read the discussion between Malcolm and Macduff we are still horrified at the butchery of Macduff's family which we have witnessed but of which Macduff is still ignorant; and, when we are reading or seeing the play for a second time, we can anticipate the mental collapse of Lady Macbeth in the following scene.

CHARACTER REVEALED IN THE PASSAGE

In the lines leading up to line 31, Macduff, although more impetuous than Malcolm, is forced on to the defensive: 'I am not treacherous' (line 18) and 'I have lost my hopes' (line 24). He is hurt and dejected that Malcolm can question his sincerity and prepares to leave (line 34). Malcolm has a measured, rehearsed way of speaking (see the balanced phrases of lines 8–10) which offends Macduff but there are reasonable grounds for Malcolm's suspicions: why has Macduff left his family undefended if he so detests Macbeth? If, as he claims, Macduff has deserted and defied Macbeth out of love for his country, how far will he go to replace Macbeth? Malcolm tests him by presenting himself as more evil than the tyrannical Macbeth and as determined to ruin Scotland even further. Macduff, so eager for Macbeth to be deposed, tries to accommodate the claimed wickedness of Malcolm, believing that he cannot possibly be worse. When Malcolm finally persuades him of his villainy, Macduff breaks from him in despair: 'O Scotland, Scotland!' (line 100). Macduff emerges from the test as an honest, patriotic idealist, flexible only up to a point. We see his idealism as brave but futile because we know what he does not, that his defenceless family has already been massacred.

Malcolm pushes the wicked image of himself to extraordinary lengths until he causes Macduff to snap. The figure he presents of insatiable lechery and greed draws attention, of course, to Macbeth's unscrupulous rule. In his testing of Macduff, he reveals a political intelligence utterly different from the straightforward patriotism and decency of Macduff. However, a worry remains in our mind that behind Macduff's 'decency', he is prepared, in order to end the rule of Macbeth, to accept a very unpleasant Malcolm; Scotland, he says, has enough women to satisfy his lusts and enough wealth to satisfy his greed, if Malcolm has some other, kingly qualities (lines 89–90). What takes place between the two men is a discussion of proper kingship, the realities of political power and, through the discussion, a critique of Macbeth's misrule.

STYLE OF THE PASSAGE

(a) ORGANISATION

The passage begins with the patriotic despondency of Macduff: 'Bleed, bleed, poor country!' and closes on a similar note: 'O Scotland, Scotland!' Although the younger man, Malcolm, takes the initiative and establishes the terms of the discussion, the lines are shared fairly evenly. The passage moves through a series of problems posed by Malcolm and attempts at some solution or accommodation by Macduff. Malcolm gradually increases the challenge until Macduff can offer no more flexibility and declares his hopes defeated. In Malcolm's subsequent speech (lines 114–37), he completely overthrows the conclusion of our passage, and in a sense, concedes his defeat by Macduff's honesty, the 'child of integrity' (line 115).

(b) IMAGERY

By Shakespearean standards elsewhere in this play and in other plays, the imagery in this passage is neither dense nor very striking. The most obvious line of imagery presents Scotland as a suffering body which can bleed, weep and be weakened by wounds. The sickness and suffering of Scotland are caused by the wickedness of Macbeth which is in direct contrast with the caring and curative powers of King Edward in England, Edward being described as 'good' and 'full of grace'. A second line of imagery presents the alleged faults in Malcolm as growths or plants. In line 51 he claims 'All the particulars of vice [are] so grafted / That, when they be opened', that is, when they shall blossom, they shall produce incomparable nastiness. In lines 76–8 he says that his greed 'grows / In my most ill-composed affection', perhaps with a pun on compost, and Macduff continues this image in line 85 when he worries that Malcolm's greed 'sticks deeper, grows with more pernicious root'. Individual images tend to be rather clichéd: 'yoke' (line 39), 'pure as snow' (line 53), 'lamb' (line 54), 'cistern of my lust' (line 63), and 'vulture' (line 74). The single unusual image occurs when Malcolm says 'had I the power, I should / Pour the sweet milk of concord into hell' (lines 97–8). It recalls 'the milk of human-kindness' (I.5.15), 'take my milk for gall' (I.5.46) and 'the babe that milks me' (I.7.55), all in speeches by Lady Macbeth. As in these, the milk here symbolises innocence, humanness, nourishment, and Malcolm threatens to exterminate human decency and order and replace them with anarchy and animosity.

(c) SYNTAX AND PUNCTUATION

Unlike text 2 (above), this passage has very little abruptness or suddenness. The two men speak in turn, say what they wish to say, and do not interrupt each other. There are few exclamations or questions; one statement by Malcolm is matched with a counter-statement from Macduff. Both men, but particularly Malcolm, tend to speak in substantial sentences. More than half the lines are un-end-stopped as if the characters have thought out carefully what they wish to say. Malcolm uses 'I' fourteen times and 'my' twelve times; Macduff uses 'I' only once.

Macduff tries to see in general terms what Malcolm says very personally. He tries to defuse or accommodate Malcolm's claims of depravity. Although he claims to be a person with no self-discipline, Malcolm speaks in a rational, coherent manner. An example of his rationality is his use of lists, first of bad characteristics in lines 57–9 with eight qualities, and second of good characteristics in lines 92–5 with twelve qualities.

(d) VERSE
Sometimes the verse becomes very undynamic and lines and groups of lines can sound very prosaic. The rhythm is unpronounced for the most part, and the sound of the verse does not draw attention to itself; the concentration is on the debate between Malcolm and Macduff. We are made to listen to the argument without diversions or distractions. The frequency of run-on lines and the total lack of rhyme further undermine the individual line as a unit of verse. Each speech is like a paragraph which we have to hear whole.

PART FIVE

BACKGROUND

WILLIAM SHAKESPEARE'S LIFE

There are no personal records of Shakespeare's life. Official documents and occasional references to him by contemporary dramatists enable us to draw the main outline of his public life, but his private life remains hidden. Although not at all unusual for a writer of his time, this lack of first-hand evidence has tempted many to read his plays as personal records and to look in them for clues to his character and convictions. The results are unconvincing, partly because Renaissance art was not subjective or designed primarily to express its creator's personality, and partly because the drama of any period is very difficult to read biographically. Except when plays are written by committed dramatists to promote social or political causes (as by Shaw or Brecht), it is all but impossible to decide who amongst the variety of fictional characters in a drama represents the dramatist, or which of the various and often conflicting points of view expressed is authorial.

What we do know can be quickly summarised. Shakespeare was born into a well-to-do family in the market town of Stratford-upon-Avon in Warwickshire, where he was baptised, in Holy Trinity Church, on 26 April 1564. His father, John Shakespeare, was a prosperous glover and leather merchant who became a person of some importance in the town: in 1565 he was elected an alderman of the town, and in 1568 he became high bailiff (or mayor) of Stratford. In 1557 he had married Mary Arden. Their third child (of eight) and eldest son, William, learned to read and write at the primary (or 'petty') school in Stratford and then, it seems probable, attended the local grammar school, where he would have studied Latin, history, logic and rhetoric. In November 1582 William, then aged eighteen, married Anne Hathaway, who was twenty-six years old. They had a daughter, Susanna, in May 1583, and twins, Hamnet and Judith, in 1585.

Shakespeare next appears in the historical record in 1592 when he was mentioned as a London actor and playwright in a pamphlet by the dramatist Robert Greene. These 'lost years' 1585–92 have been the subject of much speculation, but how they were occupied remains as much a mystery as when Shakespeare left Stratford, and why. In his pamphlet, *Greene's Groatsworth of Wit*, Greene expresses to his fellow dramatists his outrage that the 'upstart crow' Shakespeare has the impudence to believe he 'is as well able to bombast out a **blank verse** as the best of you'. To have aroused this hostility from a rival, Shakespeare must, by 1592, have been long enough in London to have made a name for himself as a playwright. We may conjecture that he had left Stratford in 1586 or 1587.

During the next twenty years, Shakespeare continued to live in London, regularly visiting his wife and family in Stratford. He continued to act, but his chief fame was as a dramatist. From 1594 he wrote exclusively for the Lord Chamberlain's Men, which rapidly became the leading dramatic company and from 1603 enjoyed the patronage of James I as the King's Men. His plays were extremely popular and he became a shareholder in his theatre company. He was able to buy lands around Stratford and a large house in the town, to which he retired about 1611. He died there on 23 April 1616 and was buried in Holy Trinity Church on 25 April.

SHAKESPEARE'S DRAMATIC CAREER

Between the late 1580s and 1613 Shakespeare wrote thirty-seven plays, and contributed to some by other dramatists. This was by no means an exceptional number for a professional playwright of the times. The exact date of the composition of individual plays is a matter of debate – for only a few plays is the date of their first performance known – but the broad outlines of Shakespeare's dramatic career have been established. He began in the late 1580s and early 1590s by rewriting earlier plays and working with plotlines inspired by the Classics. He concentrated on comedies (such as *The Comedy of Errors*, 1590–4, which derived from the Latin playwright Plautus) and plays dealing with English history (such as the three parts of *Henry VI*, 1589–92), though he also tried his hand at bloodthirsty revenge tragedy (*Titus Andronicus*, 1592–3, indebted to both Ovid and Seneca). During the 1590s Shakespeare developed his expertise in these kinds of play to write comic masterpieces such as *A Midsummer Night's Dream* (1594–5) and *As You Like It* (1599–1600) and history plays such as *Henry IV* (1596–8) and *Henry V* (1598–9).

As the new century begins a new note is detectable. Plays such as *Troilus and Cressida* (1601–2) and *Measure for Measure* (1603–4), poised between comedy and tragedy, evoke complex responses. Because of their generic uncertainty and ambivalent tone such works are sometimes referred to as 'problem plays', but it is tragedy which comes to dominate the extraordinary sequence of masterpieces: *Hamlet* (1600–1), *Othello* (1602–4), *King Lear* (1605–6), *Macbeth* (1605–6) and *Antony and Cleopatra* (1606).

In the last years of his dramatic career, Shakespeare wrote a group of plays of a quite different kind. These 'romances', as they are often called, are in many ways the most remarkable of all his plays. The group comprises *Pericles* (1608), *Cymbeline* (1609–11), *The Winter's Tale* (1610–11) and *The Tempest* (1610–11). These plays (particularly *Cymbeline*) reprise many of the situations and themes of the earlier dramas but in fantastical and exotic dramatic designs which, set in distant lands, covering large tracts of time and involving music, mime, dance and tableaux, have something of the qualities of masques and pageants. The situations which in the tragedies had led to disaster are here resolved: the great theme is restoration and reconciliation. Where in the tragedies Ophelia, Desdemona and Cordelia died, the daughters of these plays – Marina, Imogen, Perdita, Miranda – survive and are reunited with their parents and lovers.

THE TEXTS OF SHAKESPEARE'S PLAYS

Nineteen of Shakespeare's plays were printed during his lifetime in what are called 'quartos' (books, each containing one play, and made up of sheets of paper each folded twice to make four leaves). Shakespeare, however, did not supervise their publication. This was not unusual. When a playwright had sold a play to a dramatic company he sold his rights in it: copyright belonged to whoever had possession of an actual copy of the text, and so consequently authors had no control over what happened to their work. Anyone who could get hold of the text of a play might publish it if they wished. Hence, what found its way into print might be the author's copy, but it might be an actor's copy or prompt copy, perhaps cut or altered for performance; sometimes, actors (or even members of the audience) might publish what they could remember of the text. Printers, working without the benefit of the author's oversight, introduced their own errors, through misreading the manuscript for example, and by 'correcting' what seemed to them not to make sense.

In 1623 John Heminges and Henry Condell, two actors in Shakespeare's company, collected together texts of thirty-six of Shakespeare's plays (*Pericles* was omitted) and published them in a large folio (a book in which each sheet of paper is folded once in half, to give two leaves). This, the First Folio, was followed by later editions in 1632, 1663 and 1685. Despite its appearance of authority, however, the texts in the First Folio still present many difficulties, for there are printing errors and confused passages in the plays, and its texts often differ significantly from those of the earlier quartos, when these exist.

Shakespeare's texts have, then, been through a number of intermediaries. We do not have his authority for any one of his plays, and hence we cannot know exactly what it was that he wrote. Bibliographers, textual critics and editors have spent a great deal of effort on endeavouring to get behind the errors, uncertainties and contradictions in the available texts to recover the plays as Shakespeare originally wrote them. What we read is the result of these efforts. Modern texts are what editors have constructed from the available evidence: they correspond to no sixteenth- or seventeenth-century editions, and to no early performance of a Shakespeare play. Furthermore, these composite texts differ from each other, for different editors read the early texts differently and come to different conclusions. A Shakespeare text is an unstable and a contrived thing.

Often, of course, its judgements embody, if not the personal prejudices of the editor, then the cultural preferences of the time in which he or she was working. Growing awareness of this has led recent scholars to distrust the whole editorial enterprise and to repudiate the attempt to construct a 'perfect' text. Stanley Wells and Gary Taylor, the editors of the Oxford edition of *The Complete Works* (1988), point out that almost certainly the texts of Shakespeare's plays were altered in performance, and from one performance to another, so that there may never have been a single version. They note, too, that Shakespeare probably revised and rewrote some plays. They do not claim to print a definitive text of any play, but prefer what seems to them the 'more theatrical' version, and when there is a great difference between available versions, as with *King Lear*, they print two texts.

SHAKESPEARE AND THE ENGLISH RENAISSANCE

Shakespeare arrived in London at the very time that the Elizabethan period was poised to become the 'golden age' of English literature. Although Elizabeth reigned as queen from 1558 to 1603, the term 'Elizabethan' is used very loosely in a literary sense to refer to the period 1580 to 1625, when the great works of the age were produced. (Sometimes the later part of this period is distinguished as 'Jacobean', from the Latin form of the name of the king who succeeded Elizabeth, James I of England and VI of Scotland, who reigned from 1603 to 1625.) The poet Edmund Spenser heralded this new age with his pastoral poem *The Shepheardes Calender* (1579) and in his essay *An Apologie for Poetrie* (written about 1580, although not published until 1595) his friend Sir Philip Sidney championed the imaginative power of the 'speaking picture of poesy', famously declaring that 'Nature never set forth the earth in so rich a tapestry as divers poets have done ... Her world is brazen, the poet's only deliver a golden'.

Spenser and Sidney were part of that rejuvenating movement in European culture which since the nineteenth century has been known by the term *Renaissance*. Meaning literally *rebirth* it denotes a revival and redirection of artistic and intellectual endeavour which began in Italy in the fourteenth century in the poetry of Petrarch. It spread gradually northwards across Europe, and is first detectable in England in the early sixteenth century in the writings of the scholar and statesman Sir Thomas More and in the poetry of Sir Thomas Wyatt and Henry Howard, Earl of Surrey. Its keynote was a curiosity in thought which challenged old assumptions and traditions. To the innovative spirit of the Renaissance, the preceding ages appeared dully unoriginal and conformist.

That spirit was fuelled by the rediscovery of many Classical texts and the culture of Greece and Rome. This fostered a confidence in human reason and in human potential which, in every sphere, challenged old convictions. The discovery of America and its peoples (Columbus had sailed in 1492) demonstrated that the world was a larger and stranger place than had been thought. The cosmological speculation of

Copernicus (later confirmed by Galileo) that the sun, not the earth was the centre of our planetary system challenged the centuries-old belief that the earth and human beings were at the centre of the cosmos. The pragmatic political philosophy of Machiavelli seemed to cut politics free from its traditional link with morality by permitting to statesmen any means which secured the desired end. And the religious movements we know collectively as the Reformation broke with the Church of Rome and set the individual conscience, not ecclesiastical authority, at the centre of the religious life. Nothing, it seemed, was beyond questioning, nothing impossible.

Shakespeare's drama is innovative and challenging in exactly the way of the Renaissance. It questions the beliefs, assumptions and politics upon which Elizabethan society was founded. And although the plays always conclude in a restoration of order and stability, many critics are inclined to argue that their imaginative energy goes into subverting, rather than reinforcing, traditional values. Convention, audience expectation and censorship all required the status quo to be endorsed by the plots' conclusions, but the dramas find ways to allow alternative sentiments to be expressed. Frequently, figures of authority are undercut by some comic or parodic figure. Despairing, critical, dissident, disillusioned, unbalanced, rebellious, mocking voices are repeatedly to be heard in the plays, rejecting, resenting, defying the established order. They belong always to marginal, socially unacceptable figures, 'licensed', as it were, by their situations to say what would be unacceptable from socially privileged or responsible citizens. The question is: are such characters given these views to discredit them, or were they the only ones through whom a voice could be given to radical and dissident ideas? Is Shakespeare a conservative or a revolutionary?

Renaissance culture was intensely nationalistic. With the break-up of the internationalism of the Middle Ages the evolving nation states which still mark the map of Europe began for the first time to acquire distinctive cultural identities. There was intense rivalry among them as they sought to achieve in their own vernacular languages a culture which could equal that of Greece and Rome. Spenser's great allegorical epic poem *The Faerie Queene*, which began to appear from 1590, celebrated Elizabeth and was intended to outdo the poetic achievements of France and Italy and to stand beside the works of Virgil and Homer. Shakespeare is equally preoccupied with national identity. His history plays tell an epic story which examines how modern England came into being through the conflicts of the fifteenth-century Wars of the Roses which brought the Tudors to the throne. He is fascinated, too, by the related subject of politics and the exercise of power. With the collapse of medieval feudalism and the authority of local barons, the royal court in the Renaissance came to assume a new status as the centre of power and patronage. It was here that the destiny of a country was shaped. Courts, and how to succeed in them, consequently fascinated the Renaissance; and they fascinated Shakespeare and his audience.

But the dramatic gaze is not merely admiring; through a variety of devices, a critical perspective is brought to bear. The court may be paralleled by a very different world, revealing uncomfortable similarities (for example, Henry's court and the Boar's Head tavern, ruled over by Falstaff in *Henry IV*). Its hypocrisy may be bitterly denounced (for example, in the diatribes of the mad Lear) and its self-seeking ambition represented disturbingly in the figure of a Machiavellian villain (such as Edmund in *Lear*) or a malcontent (such as Iago in *Othello*). Shakespeare is fond of displacing the court to another context, the better to examine its assumptions and pretensions and to offer alternatives to the courtly life (for example, in the pastoral setting of the forest of Arden in *As You Like It* or Prospero's island in *The Tempest*). Courtiers are frequently figures of fun whose unmanly sophistication ('neat and trimly dressed, / Fresh as a bridegroom … perfumed like a milliner', says Hotspur of such a man in *Henry IV*, I.3.33–6) is contrasted with plain-speaking integrity: Oswald is set against Kent in *King Lear*.

(When thinking of these matters, we should remember that stage plays were subject to censorship, and any criticism had therefore to be muted or oblique: direct criticism of the monarch or contemporary English court would not be tolerated. This has something to do with why Shakespeare's plays are always set either in the past, or abroad.)

The nationalism of the English Renaissance was reinforced by Protestantism. Henry VIII had broken with Rome in the 1530s and in Shakespeare's time there was an independent Protestant state church. Because the Pope in Rome had excommunicated Queen Elizabeth as a heretic and relieved the English of their allegiance to the Crown, there was deep suspicion of Roman Catholics as potential traitors. This was enforced by the attempted invasion of the Spanish Armada in 1588. This was a religiously inspired crusade to overthrow Elizabeth and restore England to Roman Catholic allegiance. Roman Catholicism was hence easily identified with hostility to England. Its association with disloyalty and treachery was enforced by the Gunpowder Plot of 1605, a Roman Catholic attempt to destroy the government of England.

Shakespeare's plays are remarkably free from direct religious sentiment, but their emphases are Protestant. Young women, for example, are destined for marriage, not for nunneries (precisely what Isabella appears to escape at the end of *Measure for Measure*); friars are dubious characters, full of schemes and deceptions, if with benign intentions, as in *Much Ado About Nothing* or *Romeo and Juliet*. (We should add, though, that Puritans, extreme Protestants, are even less kindly treated: for example, Malvolio in *Twelfth Night*.)

The central figures of the plays are frequently individuals beset by temptation, by the lure of evil – Angelo in *Measure for Measure*, Othello, Lear, Macbeth – and not only in tragedies: Falstaff is described as 'that old white-bearded Satan' (*1 Henry IV*, II.4.454). We follow their inner struggles. Shakespeare's heroes have the preoccupation with self and the introspective tendencies encouraged by Protestantism: his tragic heroes are haunted by their consciences, seeking their true selves, agonising over what course of action to take as they follow what can often be understood as a kind of spiritual progress towards heaven or hell.

SHAKESPEARE'S THEATRE

The theatre for which the plays were written was one of the most remarkable innovations of the Renaissance. There had been no theatres or acting companies during the medieval period. Performed on carts and in open spaces at Christian festivals, plays had been almost exclusively religious. Such professional actors as there were wandered the country putting on a variety of entertainments in the yards of inns, on makeshift stages in market squares, or anywhere else suitable. They did not perform full-length plays, but mimes, juggling and comedy acts. Such actors were regarded by officialdom and polite society as little better than vagabonds and layabouts.

THE GLOBE THEATRE,

On the   Bankside.

As it appeared in the reign of King James I.

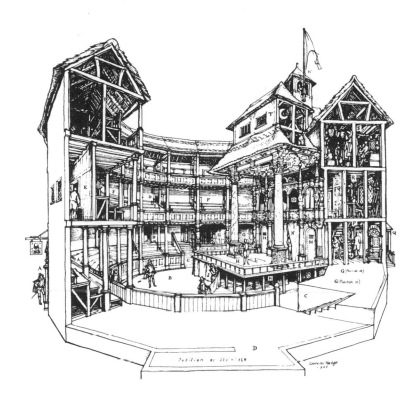

A CONJECTURAL RECONSTRUCTION OF THE INTERIOR OF THE GLOBE PLAYHOUSE

AA	Main entrance
B	The Yard
CC	Entrances to lowest galleries
D	Entrance to staircase and upper galleries
E	Corridor serving the different sections of the middle gallery
F	Middle gallery ('Twopenny Rooms')
G	'Gentlemen's Rooms or Lords Rooms'
H	The stage
J	The hanging being put up round the stage
K	The 'Hell' under the stage
L	The stage trap, leading down to the Hell
MM	Stage doors
N	Curtained 'place behind the stage'
O	Gallery above the stage, used as required sometimes by musicians, sometimes by spectators, and often as part of the play
P	Back-stage area (the tiring-house)
Q	Tiring-house door
R	Dressing-rooms
S	Wardrobe and storage
T	The hut housing the machine for lowering enthroned gods, etc., to the stage
U	The 'Heavens'
W	Hoisting the playhouse flag

Just before Shakespeare went to London all this began to change. A number of young men who had been to the universities of Oxford and Cambridge came to London in the 1580s and began to write plays which made use of what they had learned about the Classical drama of ancient Greece and Rome. Plays such as John Lyly's *Alexander and Campaspe* (1584), Christopher Marlowe's *Tamburlaine the Great* (about 1587) and Thomas Kyd's *The Spanish Tragedy* (1588–9) were unlike anything that had been written in English before. They were full-length plays on secular subjects, taking their plots from history and legend, adopting many of the devices of Classical drama, and offering a range of characterisation and situation hitherto unattempted in English drama. With the exception of Lyly's prose dramas, they were in the unrhymed **iambic** pentameters (**blank verse**) which the Earl of Surrey had introduced into English earlier in the sixteenth century. This was a freer and more expressive medium than the rhymed verse of medieval drama. It was the drama of these 'university wits' which Shakespeare challenged when he came to London. Greene was one of them, and we have heard how little he liked this Shakespeare setting himself up as a dramatist.

The most significant change of all, however, was that these dramatists wrote for the professional theatre. In 1576 James Burbage built the first permanent theatre in England, in Shoreditch, just beyond London's northern boundary. It was called simply 'The Theatre'. Others soon followed. Thus, when Shakespeare came to London, there was flourishing drama, theatres and companies of actors waiting for him, such as there had never been before in England. His company performed at James Burbage's Theatre until 1596, and used the Swan and Curtain until they moved into their own new theatre, the Globe, in 1599. It was burned down in 1613 when a cannon was fired during a performance of Shakespeare's *Henry VIII*.

With the completion in 1996 of Sam Wanamaker's project to construct in London a replica of The Globe, and with productions now running there, a version of Shakespeare's theatre can be experienced at first-hand. It is very different to the usual modern experience of drama. The form of the Elizabethan theatre derived from the inn yards and animal baiting rings in which actors had been accustomed to perform in the past. They were circular wooden buildings with a paved courtyard in the middle open to the sky. A rectangular stage jutted out into the middle of this yard. Some of the audience stood in the yard (or 'pit') to watch the play. They were thus on three sides of the stage, close up to it and on a level with it. These 'groundlings' paid only a penny to get in, but for wealthier spectators there were seats in three covered tiers or galleries between the inner and outer walls of the building, extending round most of the auditorium and overlooking the pit and the stage. Such a theatre could hold about 3,000 spectators. The yards were about 80ft in diameter and the rectangular stage approximately 40ft by 30ft and 5ft 6in high. Shakespeare aptly called such a theatre a 'wooden O' in the Prologue to *Henry V* (line 13).

The stage itself was partially covered by a roof or canopy which projected from the wall at the rear of the stage and was supported by two posts at the front. This protected the stage and performers from inclement weather, and to it were secured winches and other machinery for stage effects. On either side at the back of the stage was a door. These led into the dressing room (or 'tiring house') and it was by means of these doors that actors entered and left the stage. Between these doors was a small recess or alcove which was curtained off. Such a 'discovery place' served, for example, for Juliet's bedroom when in Act IV Scene 4 of *Romeo and Juliet* the Nurse went to the back of the stage and drew the curtain to find, or 'discover' in Elizabethan English, Juliet apparently dead on her bed. Above the discovery place was a balcony, used for the famous balcony scenes of *Romeo and Juliet* (II.2 and III.5), or for the battlements of Richard's castle when he is confronted by Bolingbroke in *Richard II* (III.3). Actors (all parts in the Elizabethan theatre were taken by boys or men) had access to the area beneath the stage; from here, in the 'cellarage', would have come the voice of the ghost of Hamlet's father (*Hamlet*, II.1.150–82).

On these stages there was very little in the way of scenery or props – there was nowhere to store them (there were no wings in this theatre) nor any way to set them up (no tabs across the stage), and, anyway, productions had to be transportable for performance at court or at noble houses. The stage was bare, which is why characters often tell us where they are: there was nothing on the stage to indicate location. It is also why location is so rarely topographical, and much more often symbolic. It suggests a dramatic mood or situation, rather than a place: Lear's barren heath reflects his destitute state, as the storm his emotional turmoil.

None of the plays printed in Shakespeare's lifetime marks Act or
Scene divisions. These have been introduced by later editors, but they
should not mislead us into supposing that there was any break in
Elizabethan performances such as might happen today while the curtains
are closed and the set is changed. The staging of Elizabethan plays was
continuous, with the many short 'scenes' of which Shakespeare's plays are
often constructed following one after another in quick succession. We
have to think of a more fluid and much faster production than we are
generally used to: in the prologues to *Romeo and Juliet* (line 12) and *Henry
VIII* (line 13) Shakespeare speaks of only two hours as the playing time.
It is because plays were staged continuously that exits and entrances are
written in as part of the script: characters speak as they enter or leave the
stage because otherwise there would be a silence while, in full view, they
took up their positions. (This is also why dead bodies are carried off: they
cannot get up and walk off.)

In 1608 Shakespeare's company, the King's Men, acquired the
Blackfriars Theatre, a smaller, rectangular indoor theatre, holding about
700 people, with seats for all the members of the audience, facilities for
elaborate stage effects and, because it was enclosed, artificial lighting. It
has been suggested that the plays written for this 'private' theatre differed
from those written for the Globe, since, as it cost more to go to a private
theatre, the audience came from a higher social stratum and demanded
the more elaborate and courtly entertainment which Shakespeare's
romances provide. However, the King's Men continued to play in the
Globe in the summer, using Blackfriars in the winter, and it is not certain
that Shakespeare's last plays were written specifically for the Blackfriars
Theatre, or first performed there.

READING SHAKESPEARE

Shakespeare's plays were written for this stage, but there is also a sense in
which they were written *by* this stage. The material and physical
circumstances of their production in such theatres had a profound effect
upon the nature of Elizabethan plays. Unless we bear this in mind, we are
likely to find them very strange, for we will read with expectations shaped
by our own familiarity with modern fiction and modern drama. This is,

by and large, realistic; it seeks to persuade us that what we are reading or watching is really happening. This is quite foreign to Shakespeare. If we try to read him like this, we shall find ourselves irritated by the improbabilities of his plot, confused by his chronology, puzzled by locations, frustrated by unanswered questions and dissatisfied by the motivation of the action. The absurd ease with which disguised persons pass through Shakespeare's plays is a case in point: why does no-one recognise people they know so well? There is a great deal of psychological accuracy in Shakespeare's plays, but we are far from any attempt at realism.

The reason is that in Shakespeare's theatre it was impossible to pretend that the audience was not watching a contrived performance. In a modern theatre, the audience is encouraged to forget itself as it becomes absorbed by the action on stage. The worlds of the spectators and of the actors are sharply distinguished by the lighting: in the dark auditorium the audience is passive, silent, anonymous, receptive and attentive; on the lighted stage the actors are active, vocal, demonstrative and dramatic. (The distinction is, of course, still more marked in the cinema.) There is no communication between the two worlds: for the audience to speak would be interruptive; for the actors to address the audience would be to break the illusion of the play. In the Elizabethan theatre, this distinction did not exist, and for two reasons: first, performances took place in the open air and in daylight which illuminated everyone equally; secondly, the spectators were all around the stage (and wealthier spectators actually on it), and were dressed no differently to the actors, who wore contemporary dress. In such a theatre, spectators would be as aware of each other as of the actors; they could not lose their identity in a corporate group, nor could they ever forget that they were spectators at a performance. There was no chance that they could believe 'this is really happening'.

This, then, was communal theatre, not only in the sense that it was going on in the middle of a crowd but in the sense that the crowd joined in. Elizabethan audiences had none of our deference: they did not keep quiet, or arrive on time, or remain for the whole performance. They joined in, interrupted, even getting on the stage. And plays were preceded and followed by jigs and clowning. It was all much more like our experience of a pantomime, and at a pantomime we are fully aware, and are meant to be aware, that we are watching games being played with reality. The conventions of pantomime revel in their own artificiality: the fishnet tights are to signal that the handsome prince is a woman, the Dame's monstrous false breasts signal that 'she' is a man.

Something very similar is the case with Elizabethan theatre: it utilised its very theatricality. Instead of trying to persuade spectators that they are not in a theatre watching a performance, Elizabethan plays acknowledge the presence of the audience. It is addressed not only by prologues, epilogues and choruses, but in **soliloquies**. There is no realistic reason why characters should suddenly explain themselves to empty rooms, but, of course, it is not an empty room. The actor is surrounded by people. Soliloquies are not addressed to the world of the play: they are for the audience's benefit. And that audience's complicity is assumed: when a character like Prospero declares himself to be invisible, it is accepted that he is. Disguises are taken to be impenetrable, however improbable, and we are to accept impossibly contrived situations, such as barely hidden characters remaining undetected (indeed, on the Elizabethan stage there was nowhere at all they could hide).

These, then, are plays which are aware of themselves as dramas; in critical terminology, they are self-reflexive, commenting upon themselves as dramatic pieces and prompting the audience to think about the theatrical experience. They do this not only through their direct address to the audience but through their fondness for the play-within-a-play (which reminds the audience that the encompassing play is also a play) and their constant use of images from, and allusions to, the theatre. They are fascinated by role playing, by acting, appearance and reality. Things are rarely what they seem, either in comedy (for example, in *A Midsummer Night's Dream*) or tragedy (*Romeo and Juliet*). This offers one way to think about those disguises: they are thematic rather than realistic. Kent's disguise in *Lear* reveals his true, loyal self, while Edmund, who is not disguised, hides his true self. In *As You Like It*, Rosalind is more truly herself disguised as a man than when dressed as a woman.

The effect of all this is to confuse the distinction we would make between 'real life' and 'acting'. The case of Rosalind, for example, raises searching questions about gender roles, about how far it is 'natural' to be womanly or manly: how does the stage, on which a man can play a woman playing a man (and have a man fall in love with him/her), differ from life, in which we assume the roles we think appropriate to masculine and feminine behaviour? The same is true of political roles: when a Richard II or Lear is so aware of the regal part he is performing, of the trappings and rituals of kingship, their plays raise the uncomfortable possibility that the answer to the question, what constitutes a successful king, is simply: a good actor. Indeed, human life generally is repeatedly rendered through the **imagery** of the stage, from Macbeth's 'Life's but a walking shadow, a poor player / That struts and frets his hour upon the stage / And then is heard no more' (V.5.23–5) to Prospero's paralleling of human life to a performance which, like the globe (both world and theatre) will end (IV.I.146–58). When life is a fiction, like this play, or this play is a fiction like life, what is the difference? 'All the world's a stage ...' (*As You Like It*, II.7.139).

PART SIX

CRITICAL HISTORY & BROADER PERSPECTIVES

SEVENTEENTH AND EIGHTEENTH CENTURIES

It is commonly held that *Macbeth* was first performed in 1606 and it has been popular ever since. It is one of the few plays by Shakespeare for which we have an eye-witness account in the playwright's lifetime. Simon Forman wrote a rough summary of the play when he saw it performed in 1611. After the Restoration and the re-opening of the theatres, Sir William Davenant redevised *Macbeth* to include song and dance routines for the Witches and he regularised, in his view, some of the language and the verse. It would have been this heavily revised version of the play that Samuel Pepys saw and described in his diary in 1667, and the many productions until late in the nineteenth century were based on substantial adaptations of the text as we know it. Samuel Johnson in his edition of *The Plays of Shakespeare* (1765) gathered together notes on *Macbeth* written twenty years earlier, in which he concentrated on a moral reading of the play and how the Witches would have been seen in Shakespeare's time: 'The danger of ambition is well described; and I know not whether it may be said in defence of some parts which now seem improbable, that, in Shakespeare's time, it was necessary to warn credulity against vain and illusive predictions. The passions [of the audience] are directed to their true end. Lady Macbeth is merely detested; and though the courage of Macbeth preserves some esteem, yet every reader rejoices in his fall.' About the same time as Johnson and sometimes after consultation with him, David Garrick, the most famous actor of the eighteenth century restored much of the text which had been altered by Davenant but also introduced some changes, for example, the removal of the Porter's scene and the presentation on stage of the death of Macbeth. Up to the end of the eighteenth century, the emphasis in writings on Shakespeare was on moral questions and on characters as representative of types of people.

In 1794 Walter Whiter published his *Specimen of a Commentary on Shakespeare*, in which he analyses the language and characters in terms of word association. By tracing the recurrence of images in a speech he identifies patterns in the mentality of a character. This more psychological reading of the plays anticipates the subtle interpretations of the inner lives of characters as practised by De Quincey, Coleridge and Hazlitt in the first half of the century. De Quincey's essay, 'On the Knocking on the Gate in *Macbeth*' is wonderfully acute on the details of one scene. Some of the best criticism was based on particular productions of the play and the acting of such famous figures as J.P. Kemble, Edmund Kean and Henry Irving as Macbeth, and Mrs Sarah Siddons and Ellen Terry as Lady Macbeth. A Scottish professor of law, C.J. Bell, wrote in 1809 a fascinating, very detailed description of Mrs Siddons showing how every intonation, gesture and movement caught a nuance of Lady Macbeth's personality. The essence of nineteenth-century criticism of the play was in examining the mystery and contradictoriness of the characters Macbeth and Lady Macbeth. This emphasis was taken up but largely removed from theatrical concerns by A.C. Bradley, whose book *Shakespearean Tragedy* (1904) analysed the main characters as if they were actual people. His study was massively influential for the first half of the twentieth century and remains very readable and rewarding.

TWENTIETH CENTURY

A play dealing with hidden desires, dark forces, guilt, sleep-walking and repressed fears could not but appeal to some of the new psychological thinkers early in the century, and Sigmund Freud showed a considerable if hurried interest in *Macbeth*. The different toughnesses of Macbeth and Lady Macbeth fascinated him and he offers an interesting suggestion that the husband and wife are really aspects of one personality dramatically presented. Although various psychological theories help to shape most readings of the play, it is only later in the century that **psychoanalytical** concepts became more central in some criticism. Derek Russell Davies's essay 'Hurt Minds' included in J.R. Brown (1982) offers an interpretation of Macbeth following on from, but also arguing with, some of Freud's categories and comments. Some **Feminist** critics have focused on issues of gender and what they see as male and female values in the play. As early as 1962, in her essay 'General Macbeth', Mary McCarthy offered a stimulating and entertaining examination of the marital relationship between Macbeth and his wife. Marilyn French, in her essay '*Macbeth and Masculine Values*' sees a struggle between male aggressive insensitive force and a softer, maternal quality which is crushed in the play. In her book, *Suffocating Mothers: Fantasies of Maternal Origin in Shakespeare's plays, Hamlet to the Tempest* (1992), Janet Adelman argues that the play is concerned with eliminating the female and trying to establish the male as self-sufficient. The Witches, in her reading, are allied to Lady Macbeth but both are disposed of by Macbeth.

The play has always been read as a struggle between good and evil, and life and death. In the more elaborate criticism of recent times this struggle has been spelled out in different ways, what might be called anthropological ways, where the values of a society are challenged or affirmed. In his books in the 1930s and 1940s, G. Wilson Knight promoted this kind of reading of Shakespeare, including *Macbeth*, where the forces of life and nature are challenged by rottenness and death. John Holloway (1961) sees *Macbeth* as 'a work which offers the spectator no view of life alone, but a view of life which is part of a view of the world' and emphasises the ritual elements in Macbeth's progression as the Lord of Misrule against Nature. In her book, *Shakespeare's Festive Tragedy* (1995), Naomi Conn Liebler also focuses on rituals and ceremonies in such elements as dress, eating, social hierarchy and hospitality.

Seeing the play in such cultural terms has an obvious connection with **Historicist** approaches. Of Shakespeare's tragedies, *Macbeth* is the most firmly rooted in the context of its original production, and some of its concerns can be seen as a continuation of Shakespeare's debate of political issues in the History Plays; this point was made by E.M.W. Tillyard in his *Shakespeare's History Plays* (1944). Henry N. Paul in *The Royal Play of Macbeth* (1950) locates the play in considerable detail in its contemporary setting and in King James's interests and problems. Relevant passages from Holinshed's *Chronicles* are included in the Signet edition (1963) and the Arden edition (1970), and the reader is able to see how Shakespeare has used one of his major sources and to ask why. Terence Hawkes offers some suggestive lines of enquiry in relating the play to such events as the accession of James to the throne of a united

Scotland and England, the Gunpowder Plot, and the colonisation of Ireland and New England, and ideas about witchcraft and national unity. Some of these contexts are explored in more detail in essays by Michael Hawkins, Peter Stallybrass, Steven Mullaney and Alan Sinfield in the 1980s and 1990s. These more recent essays can be described as New Historicist in that they demonstrate an awareness of how we read the past, of what we look for and give priority to in such a play, not just how the play fits with events of its own time.

Looking back to the attention to linguistic detail found in Coleridge's and De Quincey's interpretations, and often in opposition to the ideological or theoretical readings described in the paragraphs above, there has been a line of critics who have insisted on some form of close reading of the words on the page. In the 1930s, Caroline Spurgeon in England and Wolfgang Clemen in Germany independently developed a way of reading a Shakespeare play by tracing patterns of recurring imagery. In *Macbeth*, images of such elements as clothes, darkness, sickness and blood provided keys of interpretation for the reader or spectator. This focus on details of language fitted with the fashion of New Criticism prevalent from the 1930s to the 1960s. L.C. Knights in a famous essay 'How Many Children Had Lady Macbeth?' (1946), argued vehemently against character-study or contextual readings: 'The only profitable approach to Shakespeare is a consideration of his plays as dramatic poems, of his use of language to obtain a total complex emotional response. Yet the bulk of Shakespearean criticism is concerned with his characters, his heroines, his love of Nature or his "philosophy" – with everything, in short, except with the words on the page, which is the main business of the critic to examine.' Cleanth Brooks offers a classic example of this method in his essay on *Macbeth*, 'The Naked Child and the Cloke of Manliness'. In her essay 'A Reply to Cleanth Brooks', Helen Gardner exposes a narrowness and artificiality in detailed explication of words and her doubts are taken up by some **post-modernist** critics such as Catherine Belsey in her essay 'Subjectivity and the Soliloquy' and Malcolm Evans in his 'Imperfect Speakers: the Tale Thickens' where the assumptions of close-reading are seriously questioned.

THE TEXT AND ITS SOURCE

G.K. Hunter, ed., *Macbeth*, The New Penguin Shakespeare, Penguin Books, 1967 (revised edition, 1995)

> This is the edition referred to in these Notes. It includes a clear text, a helpful introduction, full explanatory notes

Kenneth Muir, ed., *Macbeth*, The Arden Shakespeare, Methuen, 1951 (revised 1984)

> This edition contains a long introduction, line-by-line annotation, detailed discussion of textual questions, and some of the sources used by Shakespeare

Sylvan Barnett, ed., *Macbeth*, The Signet Classic Shakespeare, The New English Library, 1963

> This edition contains an annotated text, some of the source material from Holinshed, and a selection of essays on the play including Samuel Johnson, Cleanth Brooks and Mary McCarthy

CRITICISM

Priority is given in this very selective list to collections of essays where students can sample a variety of approaches. Several of the collections overlap in their choice of essays or critics.

Kenneth Muir and S. Schoenbaum, eds, *A New Companion to Shakespeare Studies*, Cambridge University Press, 1971

> It contains useful essays on Shakespeare's background and subjects related to his work

Stanley Wells, ed., *The Cambridge Companion to Shakespeare Studies*, Cambridge University Press, 1986

> It developed out of the *New Companion* (above) but is completely revised. Contains sizeable bibliographies after each chapter

David Scott Kastan, ed., *A Companion to Shakespeare*, Blackwell Publishers, 1999

> More on the background than on individual plays. Larger and wider in scope than Cambridge Companions (above). Good bibliographies after each chapter

Laurence Lerner, ed., *Shakespeare's Tragedies*, Penguin, 1963

It offers several pieces on each of the tragedies and some essays on notions of
tragedy

John Drakakis, ed., *Shakespearean Tragedy*, Longman, 1992
The long introduction examines the whole subject of tragedy and there are several
recent essays on individual plays

John Wain, ed., *Macbeth: A Casebook*, Macmillan, 1968
A selection of writings on the play includes Whiter, Coleridge, De Quincey,
Bradley, Freud, Wilson Knight and Caroline Spurgeon

Alan Sinfield, ed., *Macbeth*, New Casebooks, Macmillan, 1992
This volume updates the previous Casebook. The introduction covers trends in
gender, structuralism and post-structuralism. The essays include work by French,
Adelman, Belsey, Evans, Mullaney, Dollimore and Stallybrass

S. Schoenbaum, ed., *Macbeth: Critical Essays*, Garland Publishing, 1991
A very varied selection of writings on *Macbeth*, including Knights, Bell and some
pieces of historical interest

Terence Hawkes, ed., *Twentieth Century Interpretations of Macbeth*,
Prentice-Hall, 1977
The introduction locates *Macbeth* firmly in events of its time of composition. The
essays include Spurgeon, Holloway, Gardner, Brooks and Knights

John Russell Brown, ed., *Focus on Macbeth*, Routledge, 1982
The essays include several on the history of productions of *Macbeth* and more
recent readings by Hawkins, Stallybrass and Davis

Ivo Kamps, ed., *Materialist Shakespeare: A History*, Verso, 1995
There is an interesting introduction to approaches to Shakespeare based on
Marxist ideas and an excellent essay on *Macbeth* by Sinfield

World events	Author's life	Literary events
1040 Macbeth kills Duncan		
1057 Macbeth is killed		
1492 Columbus sails to America		
		1513 Niccolò Machiavelli, *The Prince*
1534 Henry VIII breaks with Rome and declares himself head of the Church of England		
1556 Archbishop Cranmer burnt at the stake		
1558 Elizabeth I accedes to throne		
	1564 Born in Stratford-upon-Avon	**1564** Galileo Galilei born; Michelangelo dies
		1565-7 English translation, by Arthur Golding, of Ovid's *Metamorphoses*
1568 Mary Queen of Scots taken prisoner by Elizabeth I		
1570 Elizabeth I excommunicated by Pope Pius V		
1571 The Battle of Lepanto		
1572 Massacre on St. Bartholomews Day, France		**1572** John Donne born; Ben Jonson born
		1576 Erection of the first specially built public theatres in London – the Theatre and the Curtain
1577 Francis Drake sets out on round-the-world voyage		**1577** Raphael Holinshead, *Chronicles of England, Scotland and Ireland*

World events	Author's life	Literary events
		1581 Barnabe Rich, *Farewell to Military Profession*
1582 Outbreak of the Plague in London	**1582** Marries Anne Hathaway	
	1583 His daughter, Susanna, is born	
1584 Raleigh's sailors land in Virginia		**1584** Reginald Scot, *The Discovery of Witchcraft*
	1585 His twins, Hamnet and Judith, born	
	c1585-92 Moves to London	
1587 Execution of Mary Queen of Scots after implication in plot to murder Elizabeth I		**1587** Christopher Marlowe, *Tamburlaine the Great*
	late 1580s-early 90s Probably writes *Henry VI (Parts I, II, III)* and *Richard III*	
1588 The Spanish Armada defeated		
1589 Accession of Henri IV to French throne		**c1589** Kyd, *The Spanish Tragedy* (first revenge tragedy)
		1590 Spenser, *The Faerie Queene*
1592 Plague in London closes theatres	**1592** Writes *The Comedy of Errors*	**1592** Marlowe, *Doctor Faustus*
	1593 Writes *Titus Andronicus*, *The Taming of the Shrew*	
	1594 onwards Writes exclusively for the Lord Chamberlain's Men; writes *Two Gentlemen of Verona*, *Love's Labours Lost*, *Richard II*	
	1595 Writes *Romeo and Juliet*, *A Midsummer Night's Dream*	

World events	Author's life	Literary events
1596 Drake perishes in West Indies	**1596** Hamnet dies; William granted coat of arms	
		1597 James VI of Scotland, *Demonologies*
	1598 Writes *Much Ado About Nothing*	**1598** Christopher Marlowe, *Hero and Leander*
	1599 Buys share in the Globe Theatre; writes *Julius Caesar, As You Like It, Twelfth Night*	**1599** Translation, by Sir Lewes Lewkenor, of Cardinal Contareno's *The Commonwealth and Government of Venice;* James VI of Scotland, *Basilikon Dorun*
	1600 *The Merchant of Venice* printed	**1600** John Parry, *History and Description of Africa*
	1600-1 Writes *Hamlet, The Merry Wives of Windsor*	
1601 Essex is executed for treason	**1601** Writes *Troilus and Cressida*	
	1602 Writes *All's Well That Ends Well*	
	1602-4 Probably writes *Othello*	
1603 Death of Queen Elizabeth I; accession of James I; Raleigh is imprisoned for treason; outbreak of plague in England; defeat of Irish rebels	**1603** onwards His company enjoys patronage of James I as The King's Men	**1603** Marston's *The Malcontent* first performed
	1604 *Othello* performed; writes *Measure for Measure*	
1605 Guy Fawkes's plot to blow up the Houses of Parliament	**1605** First version of *King Lear*	**1605** Cervantes, *Don Quijote de la Mancha;* Francis Bacon, *The Advancement of Learning*

World events	Author's life	Literary events
	1606 Writes *Macbeth*	
	1606-7 Probably writes *Antony and Cleopatra*	
	1607 Writes *Coriolanus, Timon of Athens*	**1607** Tourneur's *The Revenger's Tragedy* published
	1608 Writes *Pericles;* The King's Men acquire Blackfriars Theatre for winter performances	
1609 Galileo constructs first astronomical telescope	**1609** Becomes part-owner of the new Blackfriars Theatre	
1610 Henri IV of France assassinated; William Harvey discovers circulation of blood; Galileo observes Saturn for the first time		
	1611 *Cymbeline, The Winter's Tale* and *The Tempest* performed	**1611** King James's translation of the Bible
1612 Last burning of heretics in England	**1612** Shakespeare retires and returns to Stratford	**1612** Webster, *The White Devil*
	1613 The Globe Theatre burns down	**1613** Webster, *Duchess of Malfi*
	1616 Dies	
1618 Raleigh executed for treason Thirty Years War begins in England		
		1622 Birth of French dramatist Molière
	1623 *The First Folio* published	

alliteration a sequence of repeated consonantal sounds in a stretch of language. The matching consonants are usually at the beginning of words or stressed syllables. Alliteration is common in poetry and prose, and it draws attention to and emphasises the connections between the words in which it occurs. Compare assonance below

aside a common dramatic convention in which a character speaks in such a way that some of the characters on stage do not hear what is said, while others do. It may also be a direct address to the audience, revealing the character's views, thoughts, motives and intentions

assonance a sequence of repeated vowel sounds in a stretch of language. Compare alliteration above

blank verse verse written in lines of unrhymed iambic pentameter. A perfect iambic pentameter has ten syllables with the heavier stresses occurring on the even syllables. A syllable with lighter stress followed by a syllable with heavier stress make up an iamb. An example of iambic pentameter is: 'When nów / I thínk / you cán / behóld / such síghts /' where the heavier stress indicated by ´ falls on the second, fourth, sixth, eighth and tenth syllables. If a speech consisted of line after line of perfect iambic pentameter the effect would be mechanical and very artificial. Shakespeare's skill is in keeping to a basic pattern of iambic pentameter but with sufficient variety as to give a sense of regularity *and* spontaneity, artifice *and* naturalness. Often there may be four or even six stresses in a line and the patterns of stressed and unstressed syllables can vary considerably. Blank verse was introduced in English verse in the sixteenth century and it developed into the main verse form of Elizabethan and Jacobean drama

dramatic irony it occurs when the development of the plot allows the audience to possess more information about what is happening than some of the characters themselves have. The speech of a character or even a phrase may be described as an instance of dramatic irony if the words anticipate a later development (often of an unpleasant nature) of which the character has no knowledge. When we reread or see a play for a second time we are much more aware of these anticipations and patterns

Feminist the term is used to describe a number of critical approaches which concentrate on how the female is represented in literature. There have always been some people aware of differences between male and female writers and of how women feature in literary texts but since the 1960s such an awareness has deepened and widened. More questions are now asked about assumptions concerning gender, sexuality and authority which underlie particular authors and texts written in different periods and social settings. There is a tendency in some Feminist analysis to see characters, particularly female characters, as gender types rather than as individuals; thus Lady Macbeth may be seen as Shakespeare's or the early-seventeenth-century's view of woman

Historicist the term is used to describe a number of critical approaches which focus on the social situations in which literary texts are produced, the attitudes and assumptions about values and power which are revealed in these texts, and (in the case of **New Historicism**) on what readers and critics look for and value in such texts. For example, an historicist critic might investigate how the figure of Macbeth fits with or upsets certain ideas of power in the Tudor/Jacobean state; or what an audience in twenty-first century Britain might seek to applaud in Macbeth

iambic (see note on blank verse above)

imagery an image, at its most basic, is a word-picture but in literary discussion it is used to denote the terms in which an object or person or action is described to make the described thing more vivid in the reader's mind. The most obvious examples of an image are metaphor (see below) and simile. Imagery is the collective or repeated use of such imaginative or figurative presentations of things; it can be employed for all of the terms which refer to objects and qualities and which appeal to the senses and the feelings (see section on imagery in Critical Approaches)

metaphor a figure of speech in which a word or phrase is applied to an object or action that it does not denote literally in order to imply a resemblance. An example from *Macbeth*: 'He cannot buckle his distempered [unruly] cause / Within the belt of rule'

morality play in the two centuries ending in 1600 plays were composed and performed which presented the struggle, in Christian terms, between good and evil. The plays centred on a character who represented humankind and the other characters represented aspects of temptation and encouragement in the human effort to find salvation

post-modernist a very vague term describing a variety of critical approaches united in challenging the idea that a word or a text can have a single, undisputed meaning. The author is denied any proprietorial or exclusive claim to the interpretation of his or her writing. All language is slippery and subject to a plurality of readings according to circumstances and the changing viewpoint of different readers

psychoanalytic a term describing critical approaches which are particularly interested in exploring the connections between conscious and unconscious elements in characters, the gaps between the revealed and the hidden in actions and language. The work of Sigmund Freud (1856–1939) inspired later critics to utilise and develop his theories of personality, desires and disguise in exploring how literature manifests the tensions in its creators and how it appeals to readers

soliloquy a dramatic convention in which a character, unheard by other characters, thinks aloud about motives, feelings and intentions. The audience is given direct access through the soliloquy to the character's inner thoughts. In *Macbeth* the use of the soliloquy gives a sense of extraordinary depth to the main characters and provides the audience with a perspective on the characters not available in the public actions and words of the plays. Lady Macbeth sleep-talking scene is a special development of the soliloquy

syntax the arrangement of words in their appropriate forms and proper order, in order to achieve meaning and particular effects and emphases

AUTHOR OF THIS NOTE

Alasdair D.F. Macrae was educated at the University of Edinburgh. He taught for a short time in secondary schools before taking up a lectureship at the University of Khartoum, Republic of the Sudan. Since 1969 he has been a lecturer, then Senior Lecturer, in English Studies at the University of Stirling. He has written widely, particularly on modern poetry. His books include an edition, *Shelley: Selected Poetry and Prose* and *Yeats: A Literary Life.*